The Spiritual and Educational Vision of Parker J. Palmer

HORIZONS *in* RELIGIOUS EDUCATION is a book series sponsored by the Religious Education Association: An Association of Professors, Practitioners, and Researchers in Religious Education. It was established to promote new scholarship and exploration in the academic field of Religious Education. The series will include both seasoned educators and newer scholars and practitioners just establishing their academic writing careers.

Books in this series reflect religious and cultural diversity, educational practice, living faith, and the common good of all people. They are chosen on the basis of their contributions to the vitality of religious education around the globe. Writers in this series hold deep commitments to their own faith traditions, yet their work sets forth claims that might also serve other religious communities, strengthen academic insight, and connect the pedagogies of religious education to the best scholarship of numerous cognate fields.

The posture of the Religious Education Association has always been ecumenical and multi-religious, attuned to global contexts, and committed to affecting public life. These values are grounded in the very institutions, congregations, and communities that transmit religious faith. The association draws upon the interdisciplinary richness of religious education connecting theological, spiritual, religious, social science and cultural research and wisdom. Horizons of Religious Education aims to heighten understanding and appreciation of the depth of scholarship resident within the discipline of religious education, as well as the ways it impacts our common life in a fragile world. Without a doubt, we are inspired by the wonder of teaching and the awe that must be taught.

The Spiritual and Educational Vision of Parker J. Palmer

The Birthright Gift of Self

Elena Soto

☙PICKWICK *Publications* • Eugene, Oregon

THE SPIRITUAL AND EDUCATIONAL VISION OF PARKER J. PALMER
The Birthright Gift of Self

Horizons in Religious Education Series

Copyright © 2024 Elena Soto. All rights reserved. Except for brief quotations in critical publications or reviews, no part of this book may be reproduced in any manner without prior written permission from the publisher. Write: Permissions, Wipf and Stock Publishers, 199 W. 8th Ave., Suite 3, Eugene, OR 97401.

Pickwick Publications
An Imprint of Wipf and Stock Publishers
199 W. 8th Ave., Suite 3
Eugene, OR 97401

www.wipfandstock.com

PAPERBACK ISBN: 978-1-6667-7696-6
HARDCOVER ISBN: 978-1-6667-7697-3
EBOOK ISBN: 978-1-6667-7698-0

Cataloguing-in-Publication data:

Names: Soto, Elena [author].

Title: The spiritual and educational vision of Parker J. Palmer : the birthright gift of self / Elena Soto.

Description: Eugene, OR: Pickwick Publications, 2024 | Series: Horizons in Religious Education Series | Includes bibliographical references.

Identifiers: ISBN 978-1-6667-7696-6 (paperback) | ISBN 978-1-6667-7697-3 (hardcover) | ISBN 978-1-6667-7698-0 (ebook)

Subjects: LCSH: Palmer, Parker J. | Teaching. | Learning. | Teachers. | Spiritual life—Christianity. | Christian life. | Spirituality.

Classification: BV4501.3 S68 2024 (paperback) | call number (ebook)

02/08/24

Scripture texts in this work are taken from the *New American Bible, revised edition* © 2010, 1991, 1986, 1970 Confraternity of Christian Doctrine, Washington, D.C. and are used by permission of the copyright owner. All Rights Reserved. No part of the New American Bible may be reproduced in any form without permission in writing from the copyright owner.

This book is dedicated to the memory of my beloved mother, Carmen Soto. With gratitude for your abiding love and gift of confidence.

CONTENTS

Editorial Review Board | ix
Editors' Preface | xi
Acknowledgments | xiii
Introduction | xv

Chapter 1: Who Is Parker J. Palmer? | 1
Chapter 2: A Spiritual and Religious Journey | 33
Chapter 3: The Spirituality of Teaching | 62
Chapter 4: Curriculum and the Question of a New Generation | 94

Bibliography | 127

HORIZONS in RELIGIOUS EDUCATION—EDITORIAL REVIEW BOARD

Editorial Review Board
—Jack L. Seymour (co-editor), Garrett-Evangelical Theological Seminary

—Hosffman Ospino (co-editor), Boston College

—Mai-Anh Le Tran (co-editor), Garrett-Evangelical Theological Seminary

Class of 2021
—Dean G. Blevins, Nazarene Theological Seminary

—N. Lynne Westfield, The Wabash Center for Teaching and Learning in Religion and Theology

—Maureen O'Brien, Duquesne University

Class of 2022
—Elizabeth Conde-Frazier, Association for Hispanic Theological Education

—Sheryl Kujawa-Holbrook, Claremont School of Theology

—Boyung Lee, Iliff School of Theology

EDITORIAL REVIEW BOARD

Class of 2023

—Deborah Court, Bar Ilan University

—Harold Horell, Fordham University

—Katherine Turpin, Iliff School of Theology

EDITORS' PREFACE

PARKER J. PALMER IS without a doubt one of the most influential thinkers of our time. A teacher at heart, a philosopher of education, a public intellectual, a spiritual guide. Works such as *To Know as We Are Known: Education as a Spiritual Journey*, *The Courage to Teach: Exploring the Inner Landscape of a Teacher's Life*, and *A Hidden Wholeness: The Journey Toward an Undivided Life* occupy prominent places in our libraries. The lives of countless people, many of them educators, have been profoundly transformed upon encountering his inspiring writings. Those who have met Parker Palmer in person or have listened to him speak often attest that what he writes is an expression of his own quest for authenticity and wholeness.

In 2010 Dr. Elena Soto visited Parker Palmer in Madison, WI and spent some time in conversation with him. She had read his works. This double encounter, the person and his writings, proved transformational. As a religious educator, she was interested not only in his ideas, but also in the person. What are ideas without the experiences, the people and the circumstances that prompt them? She went on to tracing Parker's own journey of authenticity and wholeness. Dr. Soto's study of Parker Palmer as a person and as an educational thinker became the focus of her doctoral dissertation and now of this book.

We are delighted to welcome this work as part of the REA *Horizons in Religious Education* series. It is an important contribution. There is a growing number of writings dedicated to the life and work of Parker Palmer. However, few have been written from the perspective of a religious educator. In this way, Dr. Soto breaks important ground. The book incorporates biographical elements, yet it is more than a mere biography. It highlights influences and relationships that shaped Palmer's thought throughout his life, but it is more than a mere genealogy of ideas.

Dr. Soto takes us onto a journey in which we learn that the cultivation of one's spiritual self is the key to authenticity and wholeness. Furthermore, the cultivation of one's spiritual self has the potential to renew the art of teaching, the way we develop curriculum and even how one envisions the entire educational experience. As a religious education scholar, Dr. Soto does not hesitate to invite us to draw from the wealth of resources within our faith traditions to strengthen the ways we pass on the faith, particularly among the new generations that seek inspiration and answers to the complex questions defining their lives in our day.

That same year (2010) when Dr. Soto met with Parker Palmer, the Religious Education Association honored him with the William Rainey Harper Award, presented to individuals whose public and scholarly work has made a significant impact on the theory and practice of religious education. Palmer's influential work, grounded in a commitment to nurturing one's spiritual life for the sake of wholeness and authenticity, is a true reminder that faith communities and our society need religious educators reflecting creatively to renew the world as well as the way we teach while inspired by the faith values that sustain us and our families.

We invite you to read this book as a practice of encounter. Meet Parker Palmer through the eyes of a religious educator. Meet Dr. Elena Soto as a scholar searching for authenticity and wholeness. The book is as much about Palmer as it is about Dr. Soto. This is a work about what we do as religious educators and why we do it.

— HOSFFMAN OSPINO, Boston College, Boston, Massachusetts. Co-chair, Horizons Editorial Board

— MAI-ANH LE TRAN, Garrett-Evangelical Theological Seminary, Evanston, Illinois. Co-chair, Horizons Editorial Board

— ELIZABETH CONDE-FRAZIER, Association for Hispanic Theological Education (AETH) Orlando, Florida. Co-chair, Horizons Editorial Board

— JACK L. SEYMOUR, Professor Emeritus, Garrett-Evangelical Theological Seminary, Evanston, Illinois. Co-chair, Horizons Editorial Board

ACKNOWLEDGMENTS

First and foremost, I want to express my gratitude to Maureen O'Brien for helping me to find the words to complete this project. Without her unwavering dedication and encouragement, this book would not have been published. I also must thank Kieran Scott, my mentor, teacher, and friend. Thank you for introducing me to the work of Parker Palmer, and for strongly suggesting that I write my dissertation based on his life and work. Without your initial guidance, this work would not exist. Thank you Parker Palmer. Meeting you and interviewing you are among the highlights of my academic career. Thank you Jack Seymour for your thoughts, and encouragement. Last but never least, I thank my brother Luis, and my sister Nereida for their love and presence throughout this journey.

INTRODUCTION

Rabbi Zusya, when he was an old man said, "In the coming world, they will not ask me: 'Why were you not Moses?' They will ask me: 'Why were you not Zusya?'"[1]

THIS STORY, OFTEN QUOTED by Parker Palmer, captures the essence of his life-long work to help us treasure who we are, to honor what he calls the "birthright gift of self." He asserts that to live a divided life means to live according to someone else's rules, standards, ideals, and expectations. In living this way, in losing the connection with the self, we begin to lose our unique identity. And, he notes, as teachers it is not possible to know our students well, nor the subject we teach, unless we are truly connected to ourselves. By focusing on living an authentic life, Palmer shows us a transformative way of teaching.

Palmer is a leading contemporary public intellectual. He is a writer, speaker, teacher, and activist, nationally recognized as one of the ten key "most influential senior leaders" in higher education and one of ten key "agenda setters" of the decade. Palmer "inspired a generation of teachers and reformers with evocative visions of community, knowing, and spiritual wholeness."[2]

---

1. Palmer, *Let Your Life Speak*, 11. Palmer cites Buber, *Tales of the Hasidim*, 251, as his source.

2. Intrator, *Living the Questions*, xvii.

INTRODUCTION

Reading Palmer's work inspired me to make his life story the subject of my dissertation in which I asked: *Can the work and life of Parker J. Palmer direct us toward an undivided life and, in turn, direct the field of religious education?* Some years later and with further research, that original idea became this book, which owes its inspiration to various factors. Foremost among them, the journey of Parker J. Palmer is of personal interest to me. Like him, I am a teacher. First I was a language teacher, and I am currently a religious studies teacher. However, of greater significance is the fact that after reading his writings, I felt as though he had written *my* life story. Conversing with him at his home in Madison, Wisconsin, in the spring of 2010 drew me closer still to his teachings.

On that spring day, I felt as though I was in the presence of a very special person. A powerful sense of spirituality, grace, and serenity emanated from him. He spoke of his life and experiences in the academy, as well as the theories he was able to formulate about those years. His philosophy about teaching was and is based on a deeply spiritual perspective, which reveals the inextricable link between the individual's wholeness, or lack thereof, and how they teach. I came away with the conviction that Palmer's wisdom about the human heart and teacher's hidden wholeness merited deeper exploration. My goal now is to share his wisdom, which grew from his life's journey, and to show how his wisdom has helped me as a teacher, has helped others, and can also help you as a teacher. Wherever, whatever, and whomever you teach, I believe that in many ways you will find his story also to be your story.

Yet although much of Palmer's writing focuses on education, his findings apply to human interactions in many settings. I have myself changed careers from the corporate world to that of education, and have found this adaptability to be the genius of his work. He writes with great candor about the culture of the academy. In his ground-breaking book, *The Courage to Teach: Exploring the Inner Landscape of a Teacher's Life*, Palmer highlights an aspect of teaching that he views as a weakness of the profession: we often teach in isolation from our colleagues and administrators. This isolation, or lack of support, leads to a disconnectedness from our students, colleagues, and our very selves. This truth undergirds most of the issues with which I have struggled as a teacher, and perhaps you too.

For example, Palmer notes that working in a vacuum at such an extraordinarily demanding job as teaching ultimately has a negative effect on one's ability to teach and relate to our students. We become disillusioned with the work we once valued. We become wounded and lose heart. He reasons that the demands placed on teachers create a coping mechanism by which, unconsciously, we begin to live a divided life; the outer self reveals what we think the world wants us to be, and the inner self oftentimes reflects another persona. When pulled in these different directions, the tension depletes the soul and destroys the heart. Palmer refers to this depletion and destruction as losing our birthright gift: our true self.

Why? Palmer explains that the "self" manifests as the human heart yearning for community, for it is through others that all humans begin to uncover their own truth. And why do we become disconnected from others? Palmer contends that it is because the culture of education is rooted in fear: fear of being judged, of being labeled incompetent, of failure, and of not knowing. He notes: "It is no wonder that most people in public school teaching leave the profession forever, after five years of teaching. They feel overwhelmed by the enormity of the task. They feel inadequate."[3] And so Palmer's goal has been to lead teachers toward their own truth as a way to regain heart.

The ability to find my own truth is Palmer's greatest gift to me. His words made me understand that I was not alone. They also helped to assuage my fear that there was something wrong with me when things were not going so well in the classroom, or with my peers. The fear had led to doubt and confusion. I thought that perhaps the answer lay in "technique." I searched through Palmer's work to find where he would say "Do this or do that, and all will be well." I never found such instructions because Palmer is not a technician. He explains that there are no gimmicks or quick-fixes that will put you on the right path as a teacher. Instead, the answer lies within the self, he says, waiting to be revealed. It is indeed a long journey to get to the point of revelation, but one that is worth every step once you get there.

In the process of learning about Palmer's theories, I uncovered other sources that helped to deepen my understanding of his work. Other scholars either complemented, bolstered, or reaffirmed Palmer's ideas. For example, I learned that stress and tension are effects of isolation. These feelings develop from living an inauthentic life of conformity, and can ultimately manifest in the physical body. John Neafsey writes that, "We get sick in one way or the other when we are living in a way that is out-of-synch with who we really are."[4] Much earlier, Dorothy Day, American journalist, social ac-

---

3. Palmer, interview by author, Madison, Wisconsin, April 5, 2010.
4. Neafsey, *Sacred Voice*, 112.

INTRODUCTION

tivist, and co-founder of the Catholic Worker Movement, also wrote about the effects of living a divided life. She recalls not knowing that the body, mind, and soul could be brought into harmony. She notes: "It seems to me a long time that I led this wavering life."[5]

My own path has wavered somewhat too. I grew up in the 1960s, and ever since childhood I wanted to become a schoolteacher. I was seven years old when I began to play make-believe school with my dolls, sitting them up against the wall by my bed and teaching them. My sister's dolls were also included, and perhaps my brother's action figures as well. These "pupils," along with the small blackboard equipped with eraser and chalk, were among my favorite toys in our New York City apartment on 108th Street. These were the early signs of my vocational call.

Over time, my eagerness dissipated. In college I learned that school teaching was considered to be "women's work," and as a result, the wages were meager. I learned that as a woman I ought to aspire to be more than what society had dictated for me. I also learned that, were I to opt for a career as a schoolteacher, I would never be able to afford to move away from home to emulate the independent lifestyle of the strong, female characters portrayed on my favorite television shows. By the time I reached twenty, I had decided against my first love of teaching and instead pursued a rather lucrative career in media. With hindsight I realized I had traded one social dictate for another.

Twenty years later, I changed careers and became a schoolteacher. Throughout this journey I have learned many things, the most important being that happiness does not come from the setting in which one finds oneself, but from the people who enrich one's life along the way. In my previous career, those people were the ones I met in the business world, who, at least at first, listened to me, guided me, and helped me practice and develop my craft. I, in turn, supported the newcomers who joined our team. There was community. There were friendships. Our success depended on connection, communication, and encouragement. My true self blossomed throughout those years. I knew that I mattered to my colleagues and to the people for whom I worked. I had a voice and my opinion and ideas were valued. The camaraderie continued outside the office. I recall many moments of joy.

However, later on I experienced the reality of the corporate world. Not only was it unwelcoming to women, it was downright harsh and disengaged

---

5. Day, *Long Loneliness*, 85.

from a Hispanic woman like me. And when I began to work among those who had some true power in the organization, I experienced the fear that, for many, drives competition. Palmer addresses much of this in his work. My own example involved a battle for power between two men, one of whom saw undermining my credibility as a good tactic to hurt the other. It was a crude and hostile world, and one that was showing me clearly that I needed to change direction in my career. My work environment became quite unlike the warmth and camaraderie that I experienced in the earlier part of that career.

By contrast, after nearly two decades in K-12 and college education in public and private, religious and non-religious institutions, I have found teaching to be a cold and solitary journey. I have witnessed the environment of isolation that Palmer so often found in the academy and I have also experienced its effects. I felt invisible and insignificant for most of my teaching career. There are no moments that I can look back upon with fondness. My days consisted of teaching too many classes with few meaningful encounters with my colleagues or administrators. I truly missed adult interaction and feedback.

It was in graduate school, while I was teaching, that I first read Palmer's words, and ultimately learned how to navigate my daily environment with a greater sense of integration and peace.

What was it about his philosophy that brought me that integration and peace? The fact that he approaches both the person and the act of teaching in a deeply spiritual and profoundly humanistic way. This resonated with me because since my early days of teaching, I longed to be seen as the person that I am. Instead, I was made to feel that I was to be a servant to students, and that it was they, the students, who mattered, and not me, the teacher. Overall, it has seemed as though teachers are viewed as dispensable, with younger and less expensive candidates waiting to fill the positions. I have never seen or felt evidence of a humanistic or spiritual sensibility within the institutions of teaching. This is why I was captivated by Palmer's vision and approach to teaching.

Palmer's strong sense of spirituality was evident even in his early college days. This offered a hint that he would later apply spirituality to his work. For instance, as an undergraduate at Carleton College, Palmer made profound statements that reveal his underlying spiritual approach to all of life. He wrote, at the time, that religious beliefs are key to all sorts of human behavior because it is from religious convictions that humans "proceed to live, face death, and give meaning to work and leisure."[6]

Later in life, the work of the famous Trappist monk, Thomas Merton, heavily influenced Palmer. Merton's work focuses on the gift of being authentic in all aspects of our lives. Later still, the beliefs and practices of the Quakers profoundly affected Palmer. The Quakers taught him how to embody the religious message of loving yourself and your neighbor by living, learning, and working together, and most importantly, listening to others and to your soul. While Palmer's work can be appropriately categorized amongst progressive spiritual thinkers of the twentieth century, I believe that his thinking transcends those boundaries while having a particular relevance for the field of religious education in its many forms.

Palmer demonstrates how reclaiming our identity can transform the way we are with ourselves and with our students, and, in turn, can transform the practice of education. This book investigates the ways he suggests that we can gather the fragments of our lives and reclaim our true identity. The essence of his philosophy relies on an awareness of the spirituality of education. Viewed through this lens, his philosophy is based on the conviction that education should strive to foster a teaching-learning experience that encourages the development of a new world view for both teacher and student, which is, in itself, a precursor for social change.

Important to the theoretical framework of this book are the voices that are brought into the conversation. These include the work of key thinkers in the field of religious education, particularly Gabriel Moran. In addition, as religious education incorporates two distinct fields—religion and education—I include the work of John Dewey and Elliot Eisner, known scholars in the field of education, to add a balanced perspective. These scholars represent some of the sources that I used to help me fully understand Palmer's theories, and the spiritual and religious aspect of my work as a teacher. For me, spirituality is the desire and search for God. The expression of that desire manifests in the religious dimension, which is how I live my life and do my work.

The work of Moran reinterprets Palmer's theories of education through a religious lens and also allows me to place Palmer's work within the broader context of the field of religious education. Moran is a valuable source for examining how individuals come to view reality in ways that are oftentimes in conflict. He reveals the effects of language on reality,

---

6. Intrator, *Living the Questions*, xxxi.

affirming that language can either limit or expand reality. In general, religious education encompasses multiple forms of teaching and learning. Religious education, in a Christian context (and when done properly), helps to form and guide the beliefs, actions, and attitudes of individuals in a way that embodies the life of Christ. To be religious is the act of practicing these beliefs, actions, and attitudes. One of Palmer's key teachings is to strive for the gradual embodiment of the subject one teaches. There are moments in the classroom at which certain interactions with students can become the catalyst for this transformation within the teacher.

According to Moran, religious education has two complementary but differing aims: to teach religion and to teach to *be* religious. Teaching religion often refers to teaching the beliefs, scriptures, practices, rituals, doctrines, and traditions of a particular religion or religions. A religious education that forms the person into *being* religious requires an education that is "life-long and life-wide."[7] Mirroring one of Palmer's theories, Moran proposes an educational framework that is composed of the forms of family, school, work, and leisure, and constituting various stages of the human life cycle. Each form embodies in part the universal values of community, knowledge, work, and wisdom.

A key question is: Who influenced Palmer? Key among them was John Dewey. Dewey, like Palmer (and Moran), believed that education has no fixed endpoint, no termination. He also viewed education and the work of schools, in particular, as "infinitely religious," and as ways to transform society.[8] Therefore, I also bring the voices of John Dewey and that of a more contemporary scholar of educational theory, Elliot Eisner, into the conversation. Eisner is important as a champion of the arts in education. He argued that an education that varied in both subject and approach was essential to the development of critical thinking in children.

These different perspectives, along with my experience, help to answer the question that this book seeks to answer: *Can the work and life of Parker J. Palmer direct us toward an undivided life, and, in turn, direct the field of religious education?* In exploring Palmer's thought, the following chapters examine his life, his religious and spiritual outlook, his philosophy of education, and his influence on my work and on that of other individuals. Furthermore, this book explores the implications of Palmer's work for the

---

7. Moran, *Showing How*, 156.
8. Moran, *Showing How*, 156. Dewey, *Reconstruction in Philosophy*, 177.

INTRODUCTION

field of religious education and for those seeking to effect change in a larger societal context.

Throughout these chapters, I use the word "teacher" in the vernacular sense to refer to those who teach professionally as professors or schoolteachers in the classroom, aware, however, that the word is also used in other settings.

Chapter 1

WHO IS PARKER J. PALMER?

Throughout his decades of fruitful writings, speaking engagements, and other accomplishments, Parker Palmer's work consistently illustrates his devotion to uncovering how to live in a way that honors the birthright gift of self. In doing so, he learned that in honoring this gift a teacher can also transform how they teach. That was the impetus of his efforts towards building a set of practical theories that could transform one's inner life and, consequently, one's outer life as well.

    The story of how Palmer influenced my work happened over time. It began a number of years ago, while I was working towards my PhD at Fordham University. I found myself at a crossroad trying to decide on a topic for my doctoral dissertation. Kieran Scott, my Fordham faculty mentor at the time, suggested that I look into Parker Palmer's work to see what I thought of it as a possible dissertation subject. I took his advice and, as I wrote in the Introduction to this book, reading Palmer's words felt as though I were reading my own life story. I was a teacher then and still am today. Palmer's theories and his understanding of the mechanics and complexity of the academy helped me to realize that I was not alone in my struggle to adapt to the academic environment. Therefore, the decision to make his work the theme of my dissertation was not a difficult one. The wisdom that I gained from studying Palmer's work helped to breathe life into my teaching, a job that I was beginning to find suffocating. His words eventually made me better equipped to establish a sense of balance and survive because they echoed what I had witnessed and felt. Knowing that I was not alone and that I was not at fault for what was happening was a liberating experience, one that helped me move forward in my work with greater confidence. I trusted the direction in which he was leading me. The challenges that I experienced were largely in my early years of teaching, but continue to a lesser degree even now.

Those challenges involved trying to adapt to a culture that was radically different from my former career. I had been in the field of media advertising with excellent teachers throughout that career. The teachers included my bosses, colleagues, and some of my clients. My introduction into that field consisted of spending days, weeks, and months learning one-on-one with my supervisors and colleagues, while also fulfilling my job responsibilities. Teaching and learning took place both in the office and in the field. I learned by witnessing others' performances and working as a team.

As I gained experience, eventually I became an independent and successful sales executive. Though independent, I was continually engaged with my colleagues and supervisors. We shared a common goal, and that was to build and maintain a strong revenue stream for the media outlet that employed us. We each had an annual budget to meet, and to accomplish our goals we had weekly meetings as a group at which we shared our experiences, both good and bad, as well as best practices, new ideas, and solutions to problems. There was a structure in place that allowed us to dedicate much of the week to teaching, learning, and sharing. This included social time together.

One of my best memories is about how easy it was to be with my peers during and after work hours. We felt free to be our true selves. Today I connect that experience with the first two themes that Palmer developed: 1) the importance of living an authentic life, and 2) the meaning of community and the innate yearning for human connection. I often experienced true happiness at work in those days. The camaraderie also gave me a sense of community that I have not experienced since then in a workplace. Knowing that this kind of fellowship can exist made the absence of community in my new teaching career that much more painful.

However fond my memories are of the advertising world, do not imagine that I walked away from a perfect career to become a teacher. I had very good reasons for leaving the field. My focus in relating these stories is the structure that existed in that particular corporate environment—one designed to enhance professional growth and productivity. Embedded in that culture was the recognition that our goals could only be accomplished in community.

I have often looked back to compare the corporate world to the academic world and wondered if the corporate structure, which was designed for effectiveness, existed because so much money was at stake all of the time. It seems obvious to me that in our capitalistic society, money and the power that goes along with it hold much greater importance than education. This is most evident in the disproportionate salaries between corporations and schools.

The disparity between the salaries of corporations and schools was the focus of a research study conducted by Cunningham and Sperry in 2001. Their study compared two jobs that were very similar in nature: a school superintendent and a corporate CEO. The study noted that the requirement for both of these positions involved responsibilities for an entire organization, managing a large workforce, multiple facilities, and a large budget. However, according to the findings, the average annual salary of a CEO was six times greater than that of a school superintendent. Furthermore, if one adds the bonus and stock options that are available to a business CEO, on average, the salary of a CEO is twenty-five times greater than that of a school superintendent.[1] Although this study took place some time ago, those of us who work in a school environment know that nothing has changed.

Another comparison in the study was between the salary of a school teacher and a business manager. The researchers point out that teachers typically "manage" classrooms of twenty to thirty children, which in my opinion requires more leadership skills than managing adults. Yet statistics show that, on average, a teacher makes half the salary of a business manager.[2] Unlike other industries, education is a field that does not lend itself to the concept of "increased production" or profitability. Therefore, one might argue that the reason for the discrepancy in salaries in both of these examples is that what school superintendents and teachers "produce" is not quantifiable in dollar amounts.

Despite being aware of the disproportionate salaries in these two worlds, years later, while still working in media, I came to a turning point in my life. After some soul searching, I realized that from an educational and experiential standpoint, I was well-equipped to become a teacher. The skills I had learned in media prepared me for being in front of a large group, albeit not adults this time but children and adolescents. In hindsight I perceived myself as having developed and honed the courage to teach. I soon learned that this was true. That I never gave up and have remained in teaching for two decades now is evidence of that courage.

1. Cunningham and Sperry, "Underpaid Educator," 40.
2. Cunningham and Sperry, "Underpaid Educator," 41.

As I have written throughout this book, my experiences in teaching mirror much of what Palmer believes. I began in the public-school system as a substitute teacher and was perplexed by the system from the very start. First, I was hired without ever being interviewed. The paperwork that I had filed with the Department of Education was all that was required. Aside from my educational credentials, what was most important in hiring substitutes in the public-school system was the assurance that the individual did not have a criminal record. Second, I was placed in a kindergarten setting for my first job. Despite my experience and worldliness at the time, I was nervous throughout that entire teaching experience. I could not understand my nervousness because of the presumption I had made about teaching—namely, that I knew all that there was to know about teaching. When I was a student, it seemed very simple to me as I watched my teachers over the years. I always thought that as a teacher I would simply stand in front of the room, teach, and guide the class activities. To add to my naiveté, I assumed that I would be given a mentor or guide as I transitioned into teaching.

Not so. On my first day as a substitute I was shown to my classroom and introduced to my assistant. Whatever was going to happen next was up to me. No one knew much about me nor what my plans were in the classroom, nor did anyone ask. I relied heavily on the assistant because she had been in that particular classroom for some time. Later on, when I was hired as a long-term per diem teacher at a local public school, there was nothing very different about the process. I was briefly interviewed that time, given the textbooks to use, and shown to the classroom. This time there was no assistant. Once again, the rest was up to me. This became the pattern that I was to experience throughout my teaching career.

The corporate world and the field of education have been polar opposite experiences. In my early years of teaching at public schools, I eagerly sought advice and ideas from my colleagues. Very few of my colleagues were receptive to sharing ideas. Most other teachers preferred to keep their distance, and some were downright unfriendly. Was this out of a sense of competitiveness or insecurity? Palmer believes that both of these factors are continually at work in the academy.[3]

While I agree with Palmer, I also believe that the school structure fosters fatigue and burnout. The tasks of a teacher are endless and grow in number as additional work is continually piled on teachers to do with little

---

3. Palmer, *Courage to Teach*, 37.

if any acknowledgment or sign of appreciation from administration. This could account for some of the negative attitudes. Regardless of the reason, my overall experience has been one of isolation, and that feeling has been prevalent in all of the settings in which I have taught: public and private schools, religious and non-religious schools, elementary, high school, and college levels. I believe that aside from the attitude of some teachers, there is another factor that significantly influences the culture of isolation in the academy but it is one that Palmer does not directly address: the daily schedules that are in place. For example, class schedules and teaching loads vary among faculty members, making it difficult and sometimes impossible to spend professional or personal time together during the workday. Also, when teachers do meet as a group, it is often only briefly and with little consistency.

The time spent in discussion is always limited because faculty members have upcoming classes to teach or somewhere else to be. This makes for very few productive conversations, little innovation, and a very slow implementation process when any new course of action is suggested. I have also been in school environments where faculty members have trusted and respected one another, where intentions have been very good and enthusiasm levels high, but the reality of the work structure almost always kept us from engaging with one another fruitfully.

The significant difference that Palmer has made in the lives of many, especially teachers, leads to the question: Who is Parker Palmer? His upbringing, the people who influenced him, and the course of his career all speak to his identity. I have explored Palmer's journey from several perspectives to illustrate who he is and how he arrived at his theories. To that end, I have placed the important developments in his spiritual and philosophical thought within specific timeframes in his life.

EARLY YEARS (1939–1958)

The story of Parker J. Palmer begins in Chicago, Illinois, where he was born in 1939. He was raised as a Methodist in Wilmette, one of the affluent suburbs of Chicago's North Shore. He lived with his parents Max J. and LaVerne Palmer, and his sisters, Sharon and Susan. Throughout his childhood, Palmer attended public schools.

The most influential person in Palmer's life was his father, Max. He was a man of great courage, pride, and integrity, who had struggled during the Great Depression. Born to a blue-collar family, Max was ultimately able to raise his children in affluent surroundings. However, his humble beginnings and values remained with him. Growing up, Palmer felt a sense of pride in living the strong, moral values that his father embodied. These qualities were instilled in Palmer, and he came to understand that the virtue of honesty, integrity, and kindness far outweighed material wealth.[4]

Max J. Palmer's philosophy of how to be in the world served him well. As Parker Palmer would later recall, like many people during the Depression his father accepted whatever work was available. However, his capacity for hard work, coupled with his sense of integrity enabled him fifty years later to buy the company and become its chairman of the board.[5] Throughout the stages of Max Palmer's rise to leadership within the company, he would periodically have a talk with his son. These talks reminded the young Palmer that every item of inventory within the company belonged to them. These were their assets. His father would then explain that beyond the tangible assets they owned was the most important asset of all, and that was "good will." That meant delivering on your word with the people you did business with, and treating them with respect. His father devoted much of his energy towards building up good will for E.A. Hinrichs & Co., because he understood that this was the real value in his business. He witnessed the ultimate failure that companies experienced when they operated their businesses otherwise.[6]

Palmer writes that his father knew his ways were not always profitable. However, it was still important to him and "It simply made him feel good to do business in this way."[7] It was apparent from an early age that Palmer's father was his role model for what it means to live authentically. The seed for his future work had been planted and, as I would soon learn, the origins of that seed went back another generation.

While researching Palmer's early life and influences, I uncovered an important intersection of Palmer's family with another family across multiple generations. Each had a strong moral conviction about how to be in the world, and in their intersection they reinforced one another—even down to the present. The information came from an interview with one of Palmer's gifted mentees, Gregory Ellison II, founder of Fearless Dialogues,

---

4. Intrator, *Living the Questions*, xxvi.
5. Intrator, *Living the Questions*, xxviii.
6. Intrator, *Living the Questions*, xxviii.
7. Intrator, *Living the Questions*, xxix.

a grassroots organization committed to creating unique spaces for unlikely partners to engage in difficult and heartfelt conversations centered on issues of race. Ellison tells the story of his first meeting with Palmer, in which he related a moment in his family's history as African Americans in the Deep South. It is worth relating here in its entirety as it so profoundly illustrates the deep-rooted tradition that Palmer's work highlights:

> Parker had expressed interest in getting to know some young writers, activists, teachers who he could share some of the strategies that he had developed over the years, in a generativity kind of space. Parker and I communicated for a couple of months via email, and he invited me out to the house. I was sitting on his back porch and Parker asked me about my family. I shared with him that I always start in telling my family narrative with my grandparents. I began telling the story . . . that my grandfather was a sharecropper in Mississippi, and he had a run-in with the landowner. He actually beat up the landowner, and this is in the late 1930s. So, you can imagine in Mississippi a black man beating up a white landowner means a death sentence. So, my grandfather escaped by nightfall and traveled to Iowa. When I said this, Parker sat up straight in his chair and asked, "Where did he go?" I said he went to Waterloo to work in the meatpacking plant. And Parker said: "Was it Rath?! [referring to the name of the meatpacking plant in Waterloo]" I said, "How do you know about Rath?!" And he said: "My grandfather worked at Rath!" Waterloo is this big (finger snap) [referring to how small a place it is]. Parker was about seventy-four at the time and I was in my mid-thirties, and we're sitting on his back porch and we're talking about our grandfathers. So, I called my aunt, who lives in Waterloo, and I said, "Aunt Doris? Do you know this man Palmer?" And she said, "*Old Man Palmer*?" And I said yes. And she said, "Yes, your granddaddy called him '*The good white man*.'" So, I said, tell me more. Now we're on speakerphone and Parker is listening. My grandfather had a fourth-grade education. It turns out that *Old Man Palmer* [Max J. Palmer's father] taught my grandfather how to read the charts in the factory so that he could get hired at Rath. It also turns out that [Palmer's] great aunt Dotty was over HR, and she filled out the papers. From that point on, Parker and I began to call each other cousins, because our families have this unique narrative.[8]

This story reveals the Palmer family's deep sense of ethics and moral responsibility. Likewise, for Ellison it reveals a long history of the

8. Ellison, interview by author, video conference, May 11, 2019.

African-American human rights struggle to be treated as equals. The story also speaks of a shared understanding of the self and of living authentically, as both grandfathers publicly acted in ways that were contrary to popular opinion in defying the racist laws of the time. The courage to live authentically would become a focal point of Palmer's later work.

In tracing the development of his focus on living authentically, I begin Palmer's life story with his high school years. Admired by his classmates, and described as intelligent, social, and popular, Parker Palmer was chosen to be president of the Student Council at New Trier High School. However, in recalling those years, he describes himself as different from his public persona. He saw himself as quite the opposite preferring solitude rather than the social world at New Trier, and feeling somewhat uninspired about his future.[9]

Upon graduating from high school in 1957, Palmer had a clear vision of what his future held. Inspired by an advertising slogan campaign that he completed for his father's company, as well as a Naval Reserve pilot who worked for his father, Palmer was certain that there were two distinct career paths that he would follow. In his first career phase, he would become a Naval Reserve aviator. Afterwards, building on his passion for writing and talent for using language to craft a world of vivid imagery, Palmer saw a career in advertising as the logical next phase of his career.

Charlie Glasser, later the President of John F. Kennedy University in California and Palmer's best friend during his teenage years, recalls that the activity they enjoyed best was going to the movies, sitting in the back, and recreating the dialogue together. Language fascinated them both. Glasser, who frequented the elegant Palmer residence, recalled it as filled with vibrant discussions. Presiding over the exchange was Palmer's father, who always impressed and delighted his son and guest. Charlie explains that Palmer's father, filled with wisdom and a natural ability to engage them as teenagers, listened to them, and was a strong supporter even when they acted as if they knew more than him.[10]

Although Palmer makes no mention of his mother in his writings, Sally Hare, a long-time friend and colleague of his, comments that she was very much in the foreground of his life: "It was his mother who kept him grounded." LaVerne Palmer was aware of her son's intellect, aspirations, and growing popularity in the world of academia. She was also aware that

---

9. Intrator, *Living the Questions*, xxvi.
10. Intrator, *Living the Questions*, xxvii.

success came easily to her son. Hare notes, "It was his mother who was there to remind him to keep his ego at bay when he needed it."[11] Hare adds that Palmer speaks of his mother very fondly. However, his father died first, and she believes that, out of respect and as a tribute to his father, Palmer incorporated in his work mentions of Max's influence on his life.

CARLETON COLLEGE / UNION THEOLOGICAL SEMINARY (1958–1962)

After Palmer graduated from New Trier High School with what he felt was a rather mediocre ranking in his class, he was accepted at Carleton College in Northfield, Minnesota. He would later recall this as a pivotal point in his life mainly because of the influential figures he would encounter.[12] In 1958 he was mentored by various Carleton faculty members, including Ian Barbour, David Maitland, and Bardwell Smith. These faculty members would later contribute essays to Intrator's book *Living the Questions*, published in honor of Palmer's work and his influence in their lives. They emphasize that the purpose of the book was not only to honor Palmer's remarkable achievements, but also to continue the conversation on the themes that have been at the heart of his theories and pedagogy: the shape of a life of integrity, the meaning of community, teaching and learning for transformation, and nonviolent social change.

Under the guidance of his mentors at Carleton, Palmer began to grow as a student. His aspirations of joining the Navy or following an advertising career began to fade as he discovered other interests. He excelled academically, and became the first student at Carleton to undertake a double major, choosing philosophy and sociology as his areas of concentration. It was through William L. Kolb, yet another key mentor, that Palmer became intrigued with the sociology of religion. In recalling those years, Palmer recounted how he had found it awkward to think of himself as an academic. He had come from a line of businessmen and craftsmen and was the first in the family to graduate from college. He never thought of himself as an intellectual. Ironically, intellectuals made him uncomfortable.

Yet when he realized that his father's deepest values were shared and modeled by his mentors at Carleton, Palmer's life began to change. He reflects on the dramatic effects these relationships had on him, and says quite

11. Hare, interview by author, telephone call, May 16, 2011.
12. Intrator, *Living the Questions*, xxix.

simply: "I wanted to be like them." He was moved by the power of their integrity, and how this translated into a life of meaning and purpose. Most importantly, these individuals cared about Palmer in ways that helped him to cultivate his own gifts and dreams.[13]

His academic excellence earned him election to Phi Beta Kappa. And, in addition to the important mentors he had at Carleton, Palmer's academic career was further advanced when he became the recipient of the prestigious Danforth Graduate Fellowship award. The award recognized his academic achievements, and steadfast religious and moral beliefs. The award also gave him the necessary financial support for his seminary studies and a doctoral program.[14]

The life-changing aspect of this award was threefold. First, Palmer met Robert Rankins, who at that time was vice president of the Danforth Foundation. He would later become a vital person in his life, both personally and professionally. Second, the prestigious award bolstered Palmer's confidence as a scholar, a world he knew nothing of having been born into a blue-collar family. Third and finally, it enabled him to make two very important decisions that year. One was marrying Sally Hartley in the summer of 1961; and shortly thereafter, Palmer and Sally moved to New York City where he began his studies at Union Theological Seminary.[15] His ongoing journey towards self-discovery, which eventually formed the thesis of his work, is evident in his writings about these early experiences.

> Carleton College was a splendid place where I found *new faces* to wear—faces more like my own than the ones I donned in high school, but still the faces of other people. Wearing one of them, I went from college neither to the Navy nor to Madison Avenue but to Union Theological Seminary in New York City, as certain that the ministry was now my calling as I had been a few years earlier about advertising and aviation.[16]

So, it came as a great shock when his grades began to plummet inexplicably, prompting doubt about his ministerial vocation. It became humiliatingly clear to him that ordination was not in his future and that he ought to look elsewhere. In the 1960s, he left Union and went west to the University of California at Berkeley to pursue graduate studies in sociology. He was to

13. Intrator, *Living the Questions*, xxx.
14. Intrator, *Living the Questions*, xxxi.
15. Intrator, *Living the Questions*, xxxi.
16. Palmer, *Let Your Life Speak*, 19.

spend much of the sixties in these studies, while also learning the cultural norm that prevailed among the youth at the time: not to be unquestioningly responsive to authority.[17]

UNIVERSITY OF CALIFORNIA AT BERKELEY (1962–1969)

While at Berkeley, Palmer was invited to play a key role in the Bay Area Colloquium. This was a national project under the umbrella of his Fellowship with the Danforth Foundation called "The Church, the University, and Social Policy." The experience shaped him significantly. He was able to, once again, form a relationship with a prominent individual who would affect his career. This was Kenneth Underwood of Wesleyan University, director of the project, an established scholar, and a highly regarded sociologist of religion. Palmer was only in his mid-twenties at the time, and found himself amongst brilliant scholars, attending seminars, writing about topics that interested him, and establishing strong bonds within the community. He felt a sense of belonging that was glaringly missing in the academic community at Berkeley.[18]

One of the outcomes of the Danforth project was the publication of a version of Palmer's Master's thesis, "A Typology of World Views," which delved into the nature of religious commitment. Back then he was aware that religious convictions, held deeply in the soul, are what animate humans. Palmer believed that it is from religious conviction that individuals can proceed to live, confront death, and give meaning to all human activities.[19] Underwood heralded Palmer's work for the depth and scope it conveyed of his intellect, creativity, and curiosity. He was seen not only as a promising writer, but for his unique contributions to the assembly of Danforth scholars, an achievement that was far beyond his years.[20] Underwood noted that Palmer's eagerness to know more about the self was equally evident in his desire to challenge how religion was defined in sociological terms. Palmer found a need to convey the clear distinction between the church and the university as institutions beyond the mechanics of how they operate, underscoring that each institution had different missions and personified different purposes.

17. Palmer, *Let Your Life Speak*, 19–20.
18. Intrator, *Living the Questions*, xxxi.
19. Intrator, *Living the Questions*, xxxii.
20. Intrator, *Living the Questions*, xxxii.

Thereafter, whenever Palmer attended scholarly functions, he recalled hearing others refer to him as "*the* Parker Palmer" about whom Underwood talked in academic circles around the country. Forty years later, he reminisces about those days with tremendous gratitude for Ken Underwood's gracious generosity in promoting his career.[21] He also recalls that, at only twenty-five years old, he was already examining the self, and observing that it is the product of one's environment, outside influences, and the result of the choices one freely make in life. Palmer was struck by the fact that the theories he developed had their roots in his earliest work, before he even realized that this was the course that his scholarly work would ultimately follow. Palmer is critical about his writing back then and remembers one of his professors pointing out just how contorted it was. It was a time, he claims, that writing well became a life-long quest—a skill that he continually attempts to improve.[22] That he has become an eloquent speaker and writer shows he succeeded in that quest.

Although he garnered the support of notable figures in the academy, Palmer still struggled in graduate school. For example, some of the professors at Berkeley adhered to a particular approach in teaching the sociology of religion. He referred to their approach as "a reductionist, debunking orientation."[23] In contrast, his own approach to teaching was holistic. He preferred to be fully engaged with both the subject matter and the students, thereby creating a dynamic exchange of ideas. Consequently, he felt out of place in the academic atmosphere at Berkeley, and decided that he had to leave the university at least for a while. Palmer needed to reflect on whether he was sufficiently passionate about teaching to endure the process of completing a PhD.

Soon thereafter, Palmer took up a faculty position at the College of Wisconsin, and enjoyed two years of teaching. He received the "Teacher of the Year" award at the age of twenty-eight. Buoyed by this experience, he developed a renewed interest in completing his doctorate—but not at Berkeley.

At that point, Palmer was familiar with the work of Robert N. Bellah, a respected scholar at Harvard University, who later wrote the now well-known book *Habits of the Heart* (1985). Palmer was impressed by Bellah's approach to the sociology of religion, to the point that he began to inquire

---

21. Intrator, *Living the Questions*, xxxii.
22. Intrator, *Living the Questions*, xxxii.
23. Intrator, Living the Questions, xxxi

how to transfer as a doctoral student from Berkeley to Harvard. Ironically, however, Bellah had just accepted a transfer to Berkeley, and so, in order to work with him, Palmer returned to Berkeley in 1967. That fall, his son Todd was born, and Palmer began working with Bellah, who later became the chair of his dissertation committee.

Palmer's dissertation was on the role of religious symbolism in the political modernization of Colonial America, Meiji Japan, and Turkey under Ataturk. It was 1969 when Palmer submitted his dissertation to his faculty committee and began to look for work: "He was eager to go out into the world and 'do sociology' rather than intellectualize about it," said Intrator.[24] The opportunity presented itself when Elden Jacobson invited Palmer to establish a new institute with the Washington, DC, Center for Metropolitan Studies in Silver Spring, Maryland. The institute would dedicate itself to community organizing with a focus on creating racial diversity.[25]

When he was already packed and ready to move, Palmer received disheartening news from Bellah: his dissertation required "substantial revision."[26] Having committed to the new job, Palmer moved to Silver Spring, where his family soon welcomed two-year-old Carrie, whom he and Sally adopted from Seoul, South Korea. The fall of 1969 was a challenge for him with a growing family, starting a new job in a new home environment, and with the unrevised dissertation looming over him. Persevering through many late nights, he completed his dissertation in December of 1969. To this day, Palmer keeps the final note that he received from Robert Bellah. Upon reading the final revised dissertation, Bellah wrote, "You pulled the chestnuts out of the fire."[27]

YEARNINGS OF THE SOUL—AWAKENINGS (1970–1974)

Upon completing his doctoral degree, Palmer's career began to advance rapidly. In these next few years, the seeds for what would later become his great contributions to educational theories began to take form. Accordingly, this section focuses on what occurred first between 1970 and 1974 that inspired later developments in his thinking, giving shape to his innovative work.

24. Intrator, *Living the Questions*, xxxiii.
25. Intrator, *Living the Questions*, xxxiii.
26. Intrator, *Living the Questions*, xxxiii.
27. Intrator, *Living the Questions*, xxxiv.

During this period, while Palmer was immersed in community organizing, John Nason, then president of Carleton College, invited him to join Carleton's Board of Trustees. Nason felt that Palmer had a future in higher education, and that he had the ability to become a dean or a university president. However, Palmer did not accept his invitation, for the dean at Georgetown University had also contacted Palmer regarding a position with the sociology faculty, which interested him more than Nason's offer. Palmer, however, did not want to leave his community work, so he negotiated to do both, dividing his responsibilities between Georgetown University and the community by involving the students in his community work.

Though for Palmer this period in his life was filled with action, promise, and unlimited possibilities, ironically it was also the period in which he started to feel a sense of emptiness in his life. He later recalled this as a discerning moment in which he realized that he lacked a sense of his inner life, and had little knowledge about spirituality or the spiritual traditions. His Methodist upbringing had been devoid of teachings about the inner life. He never had a theology course at either Carleton or Union that delved into one's inner life. Palmer knew nothing about the inner life in all those years, at least not in the way in which he came to understand it.[28]

A book that he came upon at a used book store sparked this awakening of his inner life. While looking unsuccessfully for Thomas Mann's *The Magic Mountain*, he happened upon Thomas Merton's autobiography, *The Seven Storey Mountain*, and decided to buy it. He was enthralled by the work and eventually bought almost everything that Merton had written or that had been written about him, which in turn introduced him to a stream of mystical teachings that are woven into all religious traditions. Palmer discovered Merton's work in the 1970s and was quickly able to adapt and incorporate Merton's way of thinking into his own work, as we see in *The Promise of Paradox: A Celebration of Contradictions in the Christian Life*, published in 1980.

Merton's theories of human life led Palmer to begin to develop some of his own, often using Merton's techniques. For instance, Merton found self-examination to be important and the question of identity was central to most of his work. That exploration led him to discover what he labeled "this shadow, this double." Through the gift of silent meditation, Palmer learned to recover his true self,[29] and on that basis posited that though all

---

28. Intrator, *Living the Questions*, xxxv.
29. Quoted in Bamberger, "Monk," 53.

people come into the world as undivided, integrated, and whole beings, over time they begin to shield themselves by hiding their true nature from the world around them.

Palmer began to develop a theory about humans' inner and outer lives. He refers to the inner life as the "backstage" life and to the outer life as the "onstage" life, with each reflecting the divided life an individual could be leading. In later years he wrote, "Only when the pain of our dividedness becomes more than we can bear do most of us embark on an inner journey toward living 'divided no more.'"[30] This led him, years later, to demonstrate his theory of the divided life and moving toward greater unity and healing by using a shape called the Möbius strip, which illustrates how the inner life is continually revealing itself in one's outer life. Reflecting later about his life in the early 1970s, Palmer wrote,

> Reading and meditating on Merton's work opened up the inner life in me. I started understanding what I now call "life on the Möbius strip," the way our inner and outer lives co-create reality. And I am glad I started to understand it because I needed it so badly. So much of me was in my head, so much of me was embattled with the world around me. I wanted to bring my heart fully into what I was doing, but that felt so dangerous. As I learned about the inner life, I realized that, yes, there are a lot of places in the world that aren't safe—but if you can find safety within yourself, you can be safe even in those places.[31]

Palmer also refers to the Möbius strip as "the Quaker PowerPoint."[32] He diagrams this concept by beginning with a strip of paper. In Palmer's metaphor, one side of the paper represents the outer or onstage life.

> Here the words that describe our experience are *image, influence, and impact*—words that name our hopes and fears as we interact with the world. The other side of the strip represents the inner life or backstage life: Here the vocabulary is less anxious and more reflective, with words like *ideas, intuitions, feelings, values, faith*—and, deeper still, whatever words you choose to name the source from which such things come: *mind, heart, spirit, true self, soul, or place-beyond-all-naming*.[33]

---

30. Palmer, *Hidden Wholeness*, 39.
31. Palmer, *Hidden Wholeness*, 92.
32. Palmer, *Hidden Wholeness*, 96.
33. Palmer, *Hidden Wholeness*, 40.

To illustrate the process of how one's birthright gift of self becomes contorted, Palmer takes the ends of the strip of paper, which had been formed into a circle, and now separates them. One end of the paper is given a slight twist and the two ends are rejoined creating a remarkable form called a Möbius strip, which resembles an elongated figure eight, or the infinity sign. As one traces a line along the form, one finds oneself swiftly moving from what *seems* to be the inside, then to what *seems* to be the outside—*seems*, because in fact there is no "inside" or "outside" on the Möbius strip; "The two apparent sides keep co-creating each other."[34] While the mechanics of the Möbius strip are mysterious, its message is clear: "whatever is inside us continually flows outward to help form, or deform, the world—and whatever is outside us continually flows inward to help form, or deform, our lives."[35]

Furthermore, a different message is sent out into the world if we change the form of the Möbius strip by separating the ends of the paper and then reattaching them to form a closed circle. In doing this one produces a visual aid of centeredness. Palmer refers to this as the "shadow side," where truth lies in the middle radiating outward towards one's outer, onstage life. As the closed circle of paper connotes:

> The shadow side arises when we use inner truth as a filter to exclude anyone or anything we find challenging. Real-world examples are common: witness the divisive role religion often plays in public life, where believers on both the left and the right separate the "good guys" from the "bad guys" along doctrinal lines.[36]

In order to reconcile the inner and outer aspects of one's life, Palmer later developed an approach to communicating with the soul, which he equates with the inner life. He used the power of metaphors to reveal what people's own words often fail to tell them. He explained that in Western culture, we oftentimes seek truth aggressively, through confrontation. However, in the journey towards self-discovery, people will find that the soul is shy and needs to be given space to come forth and let its presence be known. It cannot be coerced into revealing itself.

Palmer discovered that reflecting on stories helps to create a safe space for the soul, and began to explore the role of poetry as a device to lure the soul into speaking. He later referred to this approach as the truth told "on the slant":

---

34. Palmer, *Hidden Wholeness*, 46.
35. Palmer, *Hidden Wholeness*, 47.
36. Palmer, *Hidden Wholeness*, 46.

I do not mean we should be coy, speaking evasively about subjects that make us uncomfortable, which weakens us and our relationships. But soul truth is so powerful that we must allow ourselves to approach it, and it to approach us, indirectly. We must invite, not command, the soul to speak. We must allow, not force, ourselves to listen.[37]

Poetry can be effective for this process in that it creates the safe distance that the soul needs. As we decipher a poem, we can hold personal issues at whatever distance we choose while staying focused on meaningful revelations. As Palmer notes, meaningful revelations come when the person becomes aware that in discerning the meaning of a poem, they are saying things about themselves. Whether they are drawn to or repelled by the poem or someone's interpretation of it, they are often projecting their own inner issues. If they try to understand their own responses, they may discover that their inner teacher has something important to say.

Palmer uses many poems to tell his story and has written many of his own. One of his favorite poems is *The Woodcarver*, a Taoist tale by Chuang Tzu, a Chinese master who lived twenty-five hundred years ago. Palmer particularly cherishes it for its timeless relevance to anyone in search of an undivided life. The theme of this poem is one's hidden potential, which can only be uncovered by doing away with all that distracts us from our truth. Palmer learned that clarity is the key to safety within oneself. It means having exactness and acceptance about one's own mixed nature, our light and shadow sides. He explains that clarity frees us of our entanglement in relationships that blur reality, making one believe that the problems of others are also ours to solve. Palmer notes that when he became clearer about the world, he could start to have what the woodcarver calls "live encounters," meaning the ability to see others in the light of truth—one's own truth as well as the other's.[38]

PENDLE HILL (1974–1985)

The most expansive spiritual period in Palmer's life was during his years at Pendle Hill, a Quaker living-learning community outside of Philadelphia. It was there that the seeds of his spiritual awakening began to blossom,

---

37. Palmer, *Hidden Wholeness*, 92.
38. Intrator, *Living the Questions*, xxxv.

there that he experienced the nature of the true self. Those experiences became the foundation of his theories.

A deep inner searching led Parker and Sally to Pendle Hill. For years they had talked about living in an intentional community, whether by moving into an existing community or by creating one with their friends. As the years passed, they grew older, their family grew larger, and their seeming fantasy became a source of frustration instead of energy. In a co-authored essay, the Palmers wrote,

> The need for community came from our feelings of isolation and fragmentation both at work and at home. Sally's concerns revolved around the difficulties of raising three children in suburban seclusion, and of forming purposeful relations with other adults amidst the logistical chaos of a family of five. Parker's needs came from the lack of community in academic life . . . Together we felt a need for community to simplify and integrate the disparate pieces of our lives.[39]

After having visited several intentional communities, in the fall of 1974 Palmer took a year-long sabbatical from Georgetown University and moved his family to Pendle Hill. There they experienced a shared life, along with seventy others, that included daily worship, study, physical work, common meals, and recreation. A year later, Palmer resigned his position with Georgetown and became dean of studies at Pendle Hill. Sally became a crafts teacher and Pendle Hill became their home and life for the next decade.

Palmer's vocation began to emerge through a series of experiences that took him from darkness into the light of what would be his true calling. However, these were also the years when he experienced his first bout with a debilitating clinical depression. The community at Pendle Hill proved invaluable during these dark periods in his life.

Palmer described the yearnings that led him to leave Georgetown and move to Pendle Hill as a command that emanated from his heart and soul. He would go there to become dean without any time constraints, as there was no contract delineating a beginning or end of his period in that position. He thought of it as a place where his inner needs would be understood

---

39. Palmer, *The Promise of Paradox*, 59. The original, co-authored 1980 essay from which Palmer quoted was Parker J. Palmer and Sally Palmer, "The Meaning of Community: An Exploration into the Spirituality of Community" (no publication information available).

and honored, unlike any university setting that he had experienced. Fortunately, Palmer would later write that at Pendle Hill "I had found many people who knew what I was talking about a lot better than I did."[40] He also recalls that when he arrived there, he knew next to nothing about Quakerism, a fact that might seem odd given his background in theological studies and in sociology of religion. However, he notes that it is not particularly odd to be uninformed about the Quakers because theirs is a tradition steeped in practice, their preference being to communicate through action rather than public verbalization of their beliefs.

One of the most profound learning experiences for Palmer came in the form of the Quaker practice called "meeting for worship," a daily forty-minute period of communal silence. These periods were awkward for Palmer at first. When words were used, they differed from what he was accustomed to hearing in church. "I remember, for example, one fine spring morning in the barn, with the windows wide open, when a particularly vocal bird broke into extended song. It was not long before a dear friend whom I came to love, rose to speak about the 'bird within.'"[41] Palmer found this both perplexing and unnerving and began to talk and write about it. He wrote a paper that questioned the Quaker concept of the inner journey, criticizing their practice as evading the world's problems, which he suggested could lead to an obsession with oneself. He felt that the community was living under the fantasy that they were doing God's will.[42]

However, as he self-deprecatingly notes:

> Fortunately, Pendle Hill was a community full of people who knew how to invite a malcontented lip-flapper into a friendly conversation. With great patience, they helped me see that while my concerns did have some merit, they might not be the whole story. Something else was going on with me, and these Friends helped me embrace it.[43]

Palmer came to understand that he perceived the silence of meeting for worship as a threat; he felt as if all of the beliefs and practices that he had upheld since childhood were collapsing. He realized that his beliefs had been handed down to him instead of having grown from grounded, lived experiences. Until Pendle Hill, worship for Palmer had been about hearing

40. Intrator, *Living the Questions*, xxxvii.
41. Palmer, "Great People to Be Gathered."
42. Palmer, "Great People to Be Gathered."
43. Palmer, "Great People to Be Gathered."

the readings from scripture, listening to the preacher, singing hymns, and the gesture of a handshake as a token of peace. He notes, "If there was any silence, it was because someone had missed his or her cue."[44]

The silence allowed Palmer to begin viewing his life from within. He tells of a teacher once saying to him: "You will say, Christ saith this, and the apostles say this; but what canst thou say? Art thou a Child of Light and hast thou walked in the Light, and what thou speakest is it inwardly from God?" He also writes about the couplet from the British poet and songwriter Sydney Carter, "Your holy hearsay is not evidence / Give me the good news in the present tense." So, during his first year at Pendle Hill, Palmer asked himself a new and challenging question: "What can you say experimentally on the basis of your own experience? What good news arises from your life in the present tense?"[45]

At first the only answer he could come up with was: nothing. Although he was educated in religion and had read most of what was available by or about Thomas Merton, he still was not aware of having a spiritual life. It seems as though reading Merton had opened a spiritual doorway, but he had not yet entered through it. No one had ever taught him to read his personal experiences through a spiritual lens: "Belief had simply been handed down to me or had arrived through reading and thinking."[46]

Palmer later wrote that the compassion with which he was embraced throughout his years at Pendle Hill allowed him to examine his prior beliefs and practices. It allowed space so that,

> [M]y make-believe theology could collapse and I could clear away the rubble. And that same silence and compassion, along with the classes I took during my student year here, gave me the time and the tools necessary to start rebuilding my theology from the ground up, the ground of my own being. Eventually, I was able to reclaim Christianity as my own tradition by realizing that I had, in fact, experienced such key elements as forgiveness, grace, and the kind of death and resurrection that come in the midst of life. I am forever grateful for that reclamation because, as the years have gone by, I have found myself standing in need of all of those spiritual gifts time and time again.[47]

---

44. Palmer, "Great People to Be Gathered."
45. Palmer, "Great People to Be Gathered."
46. Palmer, "Great People to Be Gathered."
47. Palmer, "Great People to Be Gathered."

During Palmer's time at Pendle Hill, Henri Nouwen, a Catholic priest and professor at Yale Divinity School, became very influential for him. They developed a friendship and professional relationship that would last more than a decade collaborating in teaching and writing, and sharing other interests. Palmer referred to him as a "spiritual virtuoso," admiring his wisdom and eloquent writing about the topics that mattered most to Palmer. The topics included Thomas Merton, education, and community. Palmer notes that Nouwen "quietly served as my mentor in the things I cared about."[48]

Palmer continued his study of Merton, as well as his practice of Quaker communal silence, a practice that eventually opened him to a new way of seeing himself, his work, and the world around him. The classes that he taught were for "adult seekers," whose sole interest, and that of the school's, was in finding meaning. Meaning was all that mattered, a striking difference from the world of academia that Palmer had left behind. For that reason, the school at Pendle Hill issued no grades or diplomas. This new experience enabled him to re-envision the educational system he had left behind. He began to devote a great deal of time to writing and building his theories. Palmer notes, "Quakerism and Pendle Hill gave me a different angle, a different experience and a different language to think about the teaching and learning process."[49]

Another memorable experience occurred in 1974 when Palmer noticed a small plaque hanging on a wall at Pendle Hill with an inscription from Martin Buber. It read, "All real living is meeting." This phrase inspired him to write, "Meeting for Learning: Education in a Quaker Context." In this essay he asks, "How do we meet each other in a way that allows each one of us to meet ourselves?"[50] The essay was widely read and remains among his favorite writings. He explains,

> A meeting for learning is, in the first place, a genuine encounter between persons, a "meeting" in the literal sense. In conventional classrooms, the focus is on the isolated self. The teacher addresses the individual student, treating him or her as a receptacle to be filled with knowledge. But in a meeting for learning the individual is always in relationship, and knowledge emerges in dialogue. It is not only what the student hears but what the student says back

---

48. Intrator, *Living the Questions*, xxxviii.
49. Intrator, *Living the Questions*, xxxviii.
50. Intrator, *Living the Questions*, xxxiv.

that counts. Here, learning happens *between* persons and not simply *within* the learner.[51]

This essay contains the threads that became crucial in his later work: the importance of living an authentic, integrated life; the centrality of community; teaching in ways that lead to transformation; and education for nonviolent social change. At the core of his world view is that everything we do emerges from what we hold inside. The way we are in the world mirrors what lies within us. Our inner condition becomes apparent in the way we relate to the work we do, and those with whom we work. The inner condition also reveals how we are with ourselves. His belief in the utter sanctity and importance of the human soul is a radical premise, especially in the Western culture where most individuals grow up with a secular, spiritually void notion of human development.

The Quaker lifestyle did much to enhance Palmer's sense of spirituality and interconnectedness, particularly the "hidden curriculum of equality" that permeates all Quaker activities and therefore also life at Pendle Hill. That everything was shared and everyone valued equally was evident in the fact that everyone earned the same base salary, everyone had daily jobs, and everyone engaged in the heavier jobs together.

Palmer's routine assignment was to wash the dishes after lunch. However, as dean of studies he had a number of responsibilities outside of the community, such as attending meetings, lecturing, and raising funds. But for every day that he was off campus doing his other work, Palmer was responsible for finding a substitute for his lunchtime dish-washing duty. When he returned, he would have to compensate the other person by doing their job in addition to his own for the same number of days that he had been relieved of his duties.[52] Through such experiences, he recalls,

> [T]his hidden curriculum slowly did its leveling job on me. I came to value people more for their gifts than for their rank or status. I became more perceptive about the wide variety of human gifts, with some people shining in class, some on a challenging work project, some in meeting for business as we untangled knotty problems, some in the simple acts of kindness they doled out every day.[53]

---

51. Palmer, "Meeting for Learning," 8.
52. Palmer, "Great People to Be Gathered."
53. Palmer, "Great People to Be Gathered."

Challenged by these dynamics and how different they were from his earlier experiences, inwardly he reacted quite negatively at times. However, in looking back, he recognized the value of this curriculum and referred to it as "one of the best parts of Pendle Hill in [my] education. . . . Since I am a white male with a good education who has long been surrounded by privilege, it is not hard to figure out what one of my shadows might be and is: an overweening sense of entitlement."[54]

Pendle Hill did not completely erase this "shadow side" of Palmer but, as he explains,

> [I am] at least thinking it less often, than I would have had I never come to Pendle Hill. A sense of entitlement, I have learned, is a crimped and cramped form of self-imprisonment. I am grateful to Pendle Hill's hidden curriculum for helping me realize that the door to that cell is unlocked.[55]

As a student, the classes that Palmer attended at Pendle Hill were also an important part of what led him to reclaim himself on many levels: spiritually, intellectually, and professionally. He recalls two of the classes and their instructors in particular. One was Eugenia Friedman's brilliant poetry classes, where he learned to overcome the "bad taste" left in him by "the academic habit of chewing live poetry to death." More important, he began to find real nourishment in poetry as he uncovered clues to his inner search in the probing questions of poetry.

The other teacher was Steve Stalonas. His classes on nonviolent social change led Palmer to understand that "nonviolence is a form of deep engagement with the world, requiring more courage, more intelligence, more strategic sensibility, and a larger repertoire of proactive moves than violence ever has." This brought him to the crossroad of the inner and outer reality. That is when he began to understand what he would articulate as "life on the Möbius strip." He later wrote,

> What is inside us keeps flowing out into the world, and what is outside us keeps flowing in. Whether we know it or not, we are continually engaged in a process of co-creating reality—inwardly and outwardly and with one another. As I stand at the point of co-creation on the Möbius strip, where inner and outer continually merge to and co-create, how can I make the best possible choices about that exchange, choices that are on balance more life-giving

---

54. Palmer, "Great People to Be Gathered."
55. Palmer, "Great People to Be Gathered."

than death-dealing? In this moment and in this place, how can I help to co-create something of heaven on Earth instead of adding to the hellish mess?[56]

By 1985, he had completed eleven years at Pendle Hill. At that point, he was asked to duplicate the model of Pendle Hill at a center in Madison, Wisconsin. He and his wife, Sally, accepted the challenge, and this became their work for the next three years. During that period, Palmer experienced a second bout with clinical depression, which had a devastating effect on his marriage. Intrator writes, "After some years of struggle, Parker and Sally separated and, three years later, were divorced."[57]

PUTTING WHEELS ON IDEAS: FROM THEORY TO ACTION (1987–PRESENT)

Palmer gradually recovered from his depression. He resumed his work with the help of a grant from the Lilly Endowment, of which his mentor and friend, Robert W. Lynn, had become vice president. Palmer began to write and lecture at college campuses. Aided by the strong appeal of his book *To Know as We Are Known: Education as a Spiritual Journey* (1993), he began to receive speaking invitations from various sources, including colleges and foundations. "They found his message honest and hopeful because he offered both a diagnosis and a prescription."[58]

Palmer offered not only a thought-provoking analysis of the central problem that plagues the academy but a unique approach to the solution. He spoke about the isolation that many in higher education experience, calling its effects the "pain of disconnection."[59] He argued that this disconnection develops partly from the obsession with objectified ways of knowing that are devoid of heart and self. The objectified way of knowing distances teachers from their students and from their subjects because this mode of knowing is rooted in a fear that stems from one's belief that that which is to be known will be tainted by one's subjectivity. Chapter 3 explores Palmer's proposal for a solution to this problem. Worth noting here, however, is how Palmer's experience with communal living at Pendle Hill helped to shape

---

56. Palmer, "Great People to Be Gathered."
57. Intrator, *Living the Questions*, xli.
58. Intrator, *Living the Questions*, xli.
59. Palmer, *To Know as We Are Known*, x.

his thinking. This is evident in his vision of education as honoring the role of community in learning and a way of knowing that values human intuition, beliefs, actions, relationships, and the human body.

In 1987 Palmer's life changed dramatically. He was invited to be a plenary speaker at a conference hosted by the American Association of Higher Education (AAHE). His speech on "Community, Conflict and Ways of Knowing," earned him national recognition. The speech was published in *Change* magazine and won a 1988 national Educational Press Association Distinguished Achievement Award. *The New York Times,* among other newspapers and magazines, featured articles about it, catapulting him into the national spotlight.

Despite this acknowledgment, Palmer considered events in his personal life to be far more important. In 1992, he married Sharon Craven, who also became his work partner and collaborator in the program, *The Courage to Teach.* The opportunity to create *The Courage to Teach* had begun in 1991. Palmer and Robert Lehman, who had been friends and colleagues for many years, were in conversation. As the newly appointed president of the Fetzer Institute, Lehman was responsible for the Institute's projects, which focused on the mind-body-spirit connections in medicine and science. The project included the widely recognized Bill Moyers national public television series on the subject.

As the new leader of the Fetzer Institute, Lehman was interested in exploring new avenues for the theme. He contacted Palmer to say, "This is an important agenda and I think it's right down your alley because it combines the inner life with the outer life, and education is in the mix as well. We want to expand our mission beyond the field of medicine. Let's talk."[60] Shortly after that invitation, Palmer became senior advisor to the president, a key conversation partner in expanding the Institute's mission. Later he assumed responsibility for developing Fetzer's first step beyond medicine, into the realm of public-school education.

Initially, Palmer suggested that they expand to include the inner lives of teachers and learners in higher education. But Lehman instead proposed focusing on public education. This meant working with K-12 teachers, a group about whom Palmer knew little, and which therefore made him hesitant. However, drawing on themes in his earlier writings, he began work on the project. In a memo to Robert Lehman, which was subsequently published as a Fetzer occasional paper entitled, *Reflections on a Program*

---

60. Palmer, "Great People to Be Gathered."

for "The Formation of Teachers," Palmer poses the question that would become the hallmark of his work: "How can we move from this conviction about the soul-sources of good teaching into a program for the formation of teachers?"[61] Palmer later recalled the process, noting,

> I have whole speeches I give on K-12 teachers as culture heroes or as our first responders, people who are being asked on a daily basis to deal with all the problems that this society doesn't know how to solve as they pop up in the lives of kids. They are doing heroic work in many cases on that critical front, the front called "the next generation," our children, but are often being beat up by politicians, the public and the press for their alleged inadequacies. And, we felt, that's not right. They deserve support and affirmation and encouragement, not cheer-leading, not take a teacher to lunch, not another award, but a substantial program that would help them reclaim the heart to teach.[62]

In January 1994, Palmer held the first *Courage to Teach* retreat for twenty-two K-12 teachers from the Kalamazoo, Michigan area. Palmer thought that this would be a stand-alone event in which he would apply what he had learned to do at Pendle Hill and elsewhere and would see how it would all work with this new audience. The model was taken from a Quaker practice of sitting in circles and exploring ideas and feelings in communion with a group. It is an exploration into the true self while being alone together. He named this type of retreat, a circle of trust. The purpose of the circle is to create a space for the soul where people would feel safe enough to reveal their strengths, and especially, their weaknesses. Palmer believes, "There's healing power in the wound. It's the place where we connect with others, if we're willing to go there."[63]

The program was enormously successful. When the retreat was over, participants campaigned for a continuing program, citing their ongoing need for such experiences. Many of them spoke of how novel the retreat experience was and how spiritually uplifted they felt for the first time in their careers. Palmer, his wife Sharon, and Fetzer staff members dedicated the following years toward developing the program. Together, they designed an approach and a curriculum that are both still in use today, based on seasonal metaphors and employed in quarterly retreats that run about three days each.

---

61. Intrator, *Living the Questions*, xlv.
62. Palmer, "Great People to Be Gathered."
63. Palmer, interview by author, Madison, Wisconsin, April 5, 2010.

Palmer and his team members developed a fifty-page document called *The Art and Craft of Formation*. It articulates the principles and practices of the retreat program and serves as a template from which new facilitators can draw. They had also identified a group of individuals that they felt were the best candidates to serve as facilitators. Among them were Sally Hare and Rick and Marcy Jackson. The program was replicated, and the Fetzer Institute tracked it through careful research. The program proved to be a success. The research showed the same positive responses as the pilot program had. The Fetzer Institute, therefore, decided to invest in sustaining *Courage to Teach* at a national level.

As *Courage to Teach* developed, Lehman soon realized that it was necessary to create a distinct organization to operate the program. The work was getting far too large. This led to the establishment under Palmer's leadership of a new Fetzer holding company called the *Center for Teacher Formation*. It was located on Bainbridge Island near Seattle, and Rick and Marcy Jackson were appointed as co-directors. According to Palmer, the *Center for Teacher Formation* was to have two critical functions: to maintain the quality of the retreat work and promote the work. New facilitators were trained to work around the country.

As the program grew in popularity, the outreach was broadened to include people of other professions. Today, the program exists under the umbrella of *The Center for Courage & Renewal* with Palmer as its founder and Senior Partner Emeritus. It operates in fifty cities within thirty states, as well as in several countries abroad. *The Center for Courage & Renewal* became a free standing 501(c)(3) nonprofit organization in the early 2000s. Fetzer had supported it for fifteen years, which was considerably longer than the three to six years that foundations usually invest in new projects. Looking back on the success of the program, Palmer observed that, "After their retreat program at the Center, they [teachers] redefine the problem and redefine their role to understand that they are enough, that they have gifts."[64]

In 1997, his ground-breaking book, *The Courage to Teach: Exploring the Inner Landscape of a Teacher's Life*, was published. As Palmer notes, the book is not about the program, but it contains some of the program's themes about identity and integrity. "Its central tenet can be applied to any role that we occupy in the world: good teaching cannot be reduced to technique; good teaching comes from the identity and integrity of the teacher."[65] As I

---

64. Palmer, interview by author, Madison, Wisconsin, April 5, 2010.
65. Palmer, *Courage to Teach*, 10.

explore in later chapters, this book and the circle retreats offer participants ways to access their inner souls, discover the causes of living dividedly, and learn to live toward greater wholeness.

Now in his eighties, Palmer continues to devote his time to writing and to the work at *The Center for Courage & Renewal*. Among his later books is *Healing the Heart of Democracy: The Courage to Create a Politics Worthy of the Human Spirit* (2011), which delves into the issues of living an integrated life as individual citizens and public leaders. He writes, "The heart is where everything begins: that grounded place in each of us where we can overcome fear, rediscover that we are members of one another, and embrace the conflicts that threaten democracy."[66]

He draws examples of courage in democracy from leaders such as Quaker activist John Woolman, who asserted that the Lord laid upon his heart that "Slavery is a moral abomination."[67] Upon hearing this message, Woolman's conviction became so deep that he began to embody the message. For example, he wore white clothing because at the time dyed fabrics were a product of slave labor. If any goods that he purchased came from slave labor, he would pay the slaves.

Woolman's Quaker community admired and respected his high moral character and supported him in his efforts to abolish slavery. In discussing his impact, Palmer also draws examples from the Quaker tradition, where it is customary for issues to be decided upon consensually, and through which members work nonviolently towards social change. Palmer refers to community and consensus as a paradox because in a typical group context, people normally adhere to what the majority favors. Consensus is also a process that most politicians avoid, preferring a majority vote. However, although it is a slow process for solving critical issues, Palmer argues that consensual decision-making ultimately works best. When people speak from their own hearts into a circle, as opposed to debating one another, the power of consensual truth emerges, it is a power that comes from inner, spiritual truth. Woolman's efforts are a prime example of this. Forming a group which he spearheaded, the Quakers presented a document to the government, which still exists among congressional documents today, petitioning for the abolishment of slavery, a full eighty years before emancipation was enacted.

---

66. Palmer, *Healing the Heart of Democracy*, 51.
67. Palmer, *Healing the Heart of Democracy*, 20–23.

Palmer also writes about Abraham Lincoln, noting that he was not a "cheerleading" president. Lincoln boldly confronted the dark aspects of the country he was leading rather than avoiding them. In *Lincoln's Melancholy*, author Joshua Shenk writes that Lincoln wrestled with clinical depression from the age of twenty. Palmer observes that the shadow, the darkness in him, is visible in his face, as in the Hebrew scripture's description of the "Man of Sorrows." Lincoln had to reconcile his dark side and light side in order to lead the nation. He had to learn how to merge the two sides of himself. For Palmer, this is an example of living an undivided life in the highest office. According to Palmer, Lincoln knew that cheerleading was unrealistic because it would have ignored the essence of the reality in which he was living as a public figure. Lincoln always acknowledged the dark and light side of the nation he was leading, holding both sides in creative tension. In other words, Palmer sees Lincoln's ability to recognize and deal with the reality of the two forces that existed in the country as directly related to his capacity to live his own life undividedly.

Healing the Heart of Democracy contains the threads that exist in all of Palmer's work. He declares that regardless of one's vocation in life, whether one is a teacher, a doctor, a lawyer, or a politician, and whether one is trying to discern who one truly is or trying to make the right decision about a critical matter, "Have that conversation [with your soul] and the results or effects will flow out to your students, patients, clients, etc."[68]

Palmer continues to explore what he has learned about the self and the world. His most recent book was published in 2018 and titled, *On the Brink of Everything: Grace, Gravity and Getting Old*. In this work, Palmer looks back on eight decades of his life and work. He shares insights and invites readers to explore their own experience. "Age itself," he says, "is no excuse to wade in the shallows. It's a reason to dive deep and take creative risks . . . The laws of nature that dictate sundown dictate our demise. But how we travel the arc toward the sunset of our lives is ours to choose: will it be denial, defiance, or collaboration?"[69]

The preceding analysis of the various phases in Palmer's life reveals a parallel with developmental psychologist and analyst Erik Erikson's theory of human life stages. Palmer's life seems to illustrate the theory of a healthy completion of each life stage, albeit with trials and tribulations. His accomplishments in his later years are most notable, as he chose generativity over

---

68. Palmer, interview by author, Madison, Wisconsin, April 5, 2010.
69. Palmer, *On the Brink of Everything*, cover.

stagnation (Erikson's seventh stage) and ultimately claimed integrity over despair (Erikson's eighth stage) in how he views his life, accomplishments, and contributions to the next generation.

CONCLUDING THOUGHTS

From my vantage point as I did the research for this book, a pattern emerged in Parker J. Palmer's life. As regards to his career, what he needed most at different times in his life tended to flow towards him rather easily. It was a pattern that his mother, LaVerne Palmer, clearly discerned early on. This claim does not ignore Palmer's virtues of hard work and perseverance but rather points to material and social advantages, such as being born into a privileged home with invested parents, which by definition afforded him unique opportunities, such as access to people who would help shape his future. Palmer's sharp intellect caught the attention of leaders and scholars, and his greatest gift was his ability to find the right people to encourage and support him. Had he not found this support throughout his career, we may not have come to know his work.

This is something that he acknowledges. In *The Courage to Teach*, he writes:

> Looking back, I realize that I was blessed with mentors at every crucial stage of my life, at every point where my identity needed to grow: in adolescence, in college, in graduate school, and early in my professional career. But a funny thing happened on the way to full adulthood: the mentors stopped coming. For several years I waited for the next one in vain, and for several years my own growth was on hold. Then I realized what was happening....[70]

It was now his turn to be a mentor to someone else and to offer others some of the many gifts he had received. Palmer saw this as a new opportunity for his own personal growth, the chance to experience the world through the eyes of a new generation.[71] As he transitioned from mentee to mentor, Palmer found support in the form of influential colleagues who stayed close to his work and who helped him bring his work to new levels. He also cultivated relationships with younger generations of leaders, two of whom will

---

70. Palmer, *Courage to Teach*, 26.
71. Palmer, *Courage to Teach*, 26.

demonstrate his impact on their work in my final chapter. Further, Palmer's legacy will live on especially in his organization, *The Center for Courage & Renewal*.

However, despite his success, Palmer continues to live with the demons of restlessness and depression. In young adulthood, his active mind led him to question his restlessness, which opened new avenues for his ways of thinking. Later, his depression led him to question the very meaning of his existence, which in turn prompted him to further his journey towards self-discovery. In the process, he found answers that gave voice to the yearnings of the soul, and through his gift of writing and public speaking he has made these discoveries available to his readers and audiences worldwide.

His readers have commented that, "I knew all of these things all the time but I didn't know how to say them. I didn't have the words for them." They've also said, "I had the words but I didn't know you could say them in public. I didn't know that anybody would understand if I talked about these things." As he heard these statements, recalls Palmer, "I started realizing that this is a huge blessing that has just been given to me. It's an exchange of gifts that in some mysterious way, I told a story in a book that helped this person claim their own story on a deeper level."[72]

Palmer's work does not offer a quick remedy to the problems we face, only a shorter distance between losing our truth and finding our truth once again. In *A Hidden Wholeness* he writes,

> I do not know who coined the phrase, "Every day, in every way, I am getting better and better," but he or she must have had a great fantasy life. In sixty-five years on earth, my pattern has never been onward and upward. It has always been up and down and back around. I follow the thread of true self faithfully for a while. Then I lose it and find myself back in the dark, where fear drives me to search for the thread once again. That pattern, as far as I can tell, is inherent in the human condition. Yet its grip on my life has weakened as I have explored it in circles of trust. Today I lose the thread less often than I once did and find it sooner when I do.[73]

In the many years of holding circle of trust retreats and in delivering lectures, Palmer often hears participants say, "What goes on here is what I

---

72. Palmer, "Great People to Be Gathered."
73. Palmer, *Hidden Wholeness*, 90.

had hoped my religious community would be like."[74] This statement reveals both the power and potential for his theories to influence how religious communities and religious educators engage with those who are seeking truth.

An analysis of Palmer's life reveals that his approach to teaching is imbued with Christian thought. As such, he brings religious sensibilities into the ideas of teaching, thereby contributing to the field of religious education in its many forms. For example, without specifically pointing to Christ (an intentional choice, as I show in later chapters), Palmer's theories emphasize what, as well as how, Jesus taught; he led *with* compassion and walked *with* his disciples, and taught them to love by loving them. Likewise, Palmer speaks of teaching as a form of "walking with" (and not ahead of) the students and meeting students where they are, without attempting to change them—each of which points to a kind of love.

Palmer's theories and approach to teaching, which are profoundly spiritual, can readily be brought into conversation with the ideas of religious scholars such as Gabriel Moran. In addition, Palmer's ideas about teaching to the totality of the person runs parallel to the educational theories developed by Elliot Eisner and John Dewey. These conversations I explore in the next two chapters.

---

74. Palmer, *Hidden Wholeness*, 75.

Chapter 2

A SPIRITUAL AND RELIGIOUS JOURNEY

WHAT WERE THE SPIRITUAL foundations of Palmer's theories? Key to the development of his perspectives was his inner search for meaning and connectedness. His journey led him to people and places that helped him uncover for what he truly yearned: to live an undivided life. He would learn that at the core of his being lay a buried treasure waiting to be discovered. In particular, it was his deep study of Thomas Merton's work that gave meaning and expression to what he was to uncover—a hidden wholeness. Although they never met, Merton's fingerprints can be seen throughout Palmer's work, as this chapter will show.

The depth of Palmer's yearning for meaning and connectedness drew him into a profound state of depression that he experienced at various times in his life. But, however dark and devastating these bouts were, they came to serve as catalysts for his self-realization, spiritual growth, and theoretical developments. Given that he uses the suffering in his life to teach others how to heal the divide that lies within oneself, Henri Nouwen's metaphor of the "wounded healer" is apropos for this study of Palmer. Nouwen wrestled with many demons in his life and learned that his own wounds helped him to recognize the suffering in others. He also recognized that as a priest, his wounds enabled him to be a more effective spiritual healer. Nouwen theorized that one's wounds have the power to heal others, referring to himself and to his work as *The Wounded Healer* (1972). Palmer acknowledged Nouwen as a spiritual virtuoso, a man who gave him the courage to show his vulnerability and to share his own wounds as a gift to others. Palmer has passed this gift along to me, which I in turn, share with my readers in upcoming sections.

Other voices that I bring into conversation with Palmer's spiritual and religious vision are those who helped shape my understanding of these concepts, and whose work either complements or corroborates Palmer's theories. First is Gabriel Moran, a renowned religious education scholar. He is a valuable source for examining how individuals oftentimes come to view reality in conflicting ways. His focus is on language, emphasizing how it can have a profound effect on the inner life. In addition, Moran views education as spiritual, life-long, and life-wide, which complements Palmer's holistic approach in teaching and learning.

Second is Catholic spiritual writer Ronald Rolheiser, who is an excellent source for uncovering the meaning of spirituality, a word that is frequently misunderstood. Rolheiser eloquently explains how spirituality necessarily affects every aspect of human experience. Further, the work of psychologist and theologian John Neafsey challenges readers to distinguish between the authentic inner voice and the competing counterfeit voices in our culture. He invites us to go inward and listen to the heart for the wisdom that resides within us and for the calling of the "sacred voice." This source provides a perspective on certain cultural pressures that lead to a divided life. Fourth is Dorothy Day, co-founder of the Catholic Worker Movement, who embodies an authentic way of living in answering her vocational call. Her experiences shape the journey that it could take to live undividedly and thus help to illuminate this concept in Palmer's work.

As I noted in the previous chapter, Palmer has claimed that in all his years on earth, his personal "growth pattern has never been onward and upward. It has always been up and down and back around."[1] This applies to his spiritual development, which he reveals as he explains his theory of the divided life. What he learned, and the lessons he applied over the course of his life, are embedded in this theory. The theory of the divided life is imbued with Palmer's sense of spirituality and modern psychological insights. It provides an overview of his perspective on spirituality and religion. As a starting point for the study of Palmer's religious and spiritual outlook, this chapter consequently offers a closer examination of his theory of the divided life, and how to move toward wholeness within a religious and spiritual context. Palmer's own journey toward wholeness began with the recognition of what was lacking in his life. The discoveries illuminated his religious and spiritual outlook.

---

1. Palmer, *Hidden Wholeness*, 90.

Palmer observes that "everything in the universe has a nature, which means limits as well as potentials . . . Making pottery, for example, involves more than the potter telling the clay what to become. The clay presses back on the potter's hands, telling her what it can and cannot do. If she fails to listen, the outcome will be both frail and ungainly."[2] One cannot change things or people at will. A healthy engagement with the world requires understanding and honoring the nature of the other, whether it be a person or an inanimate object. Even more important for Palmer, however, is to honor the self with all of one's limits as well as potentials. He believes that the first step towards living in fruitful communion with others is to be authentic.

Losing one's authenticity is a process by which individuals respond to external cues that suggest that there are better ways of being in the world than as our true selves. These external forces begin early in life and become an ongoing obstacle in claiming one's authenticity. Individuals are surrounded by images of who they ought to be and struggle with their inherent need to be seen, loved, and in communion with others. Palmer argues that society attempts to fit each of us into slots that conform to the norms and mores of the culture in which we live. He writes, "In families, schools, work-places, and religious communities, we are trained away from true self toward images of acceptability; under social pressures like racism and sexism our original shape is deformed beyond recognition; and we ourselves, driven by fear, too often betray true self to gain the approval of others."[3]

An interesting aspect of this human pattern is that while it is generally associated with peer pressure in the adolescent phase, Palmer's work highlights its continuation throughout adulthood. In the long process that it takes to discover one's deep identity, one masks oneself by putting on other people's faces. Sometimes we want to emulate others because we are drawn to them; at other times we succumb to outside pressures in order to feel welcomed by others. This is part of the human condition and also part of what it means to live in community—until you discover your true self.

John Neafsey, a practicing psychologist and theologian, correlates the two disciplines in examining this aspect of the self with a focus on vocation. His findings mesh with Palmer's theory of the divided life. In *A Sacred Voice Is Calling*, Neafsey examines the spirituality of vocation and correlates it with his findings that inauthentic living impedes one's ability to hear the sacred, inner voice that guides one. He writes, "The true self is grounded

2. Palmer, *Let Your Life Speak*, 15.
3. Palmer, *Let Your Life Speak*, 12.

in our personal emotional truth, our true feelings, what we actually think and feel about things. It is rooted in the emotional reality of what *is*, rather than in what we think we *should* be feeling."[4] According to Neafsey, the false self develops during childhood; it is learned behavior. An example he cites is when our parents or family or culture cannot or will not tolerate or accept who we actually are. When this happens, we begin to learn that it is "dangerous to be oneself."[5]

Neafsey adds, "The person develops a kind of inauthentic mask that is motivated by the need to adjust or conform to the expectations and wishes of others, either to win their approval or to avoid their rejection . . . The mask serves both to conceal and to protect the true self, which remains hidden, and, in extreme cases, forgotten or repressed within the unconscious of the person."[6] For Neafsey, vocation lends itself to a way of determining whether or not a person is living an authentic life.

Dorothy Day, journalist, activist, humanist, and co-founder of the Catholic Worker Movement, embodies the concept of living undividedly through her vocational choice. Although she struggled to be a professional woman in the 1940s, and wrestled with the cultural voices vying for her attention, she eventually found her true calling. Unpopular as it was and remains today, Dorothy Day devoted her life to sheltering the homeless and mentally ill. In her autobiography she wrote: "I had received a calling, a vocation, a direction to my life. I felt even at fifteen, that God meant man to be happy, that He meant to provide him with what he needed to maintain life in order to be happy, and that we did not need to have quite so much destitution and misery as I saw all around and read of in the daily press."[7] As she began her journey toward her vocation, she realized:

> No one was taking off his coat and giving it to the poor. I didn't see anyone having a banquet and calling in the lame, the halt and the blind. And those who were doing it, like the Salvation Army, did not appeal to me. I wanted, though I did not know it then, a synthesis. I wanted life and I wanted the abundant life. I wanted it for others too.[8]

---

4. Neafsey, *Sacred Voice*, 54.
5. Neafsey, *Sacred Voice*, 54.
6. Neafsey, *Sacred Voice*, 55.
7. Day, *Long Loneliness*, 38.
8. Day, *Long Loneliness*, 39.

For Palmer, the search for his true vocation led him to learn about how living a divided life becomes an obstacle in this journey. He recollects:

> I was in my early thirties when I started to understand that it is indeed possible to live a life other than one's own. Fearful that I was doing just that—but uncertain about the deeper, truer life I sensed hidden inside of me, uncertain whether it was real or trustworthy or within reach—I would snap awake in the middle of the night and stare for long hours at the ceiling.[9]

Some thirty years later, his understanding had blossomed into a mature outlook on vocation. Palmer learned that one should not live with a perspective from the outside in, but from the inside out. He explains, "Before you tell your life what you intend to do with it, listen for what it intends to do with you. Before you tell your life what truths and values you have decided to live up to, let your life tell you what truths you embody, what values you represent."[10]

However, before one can reach this level of understanding, one typically has to undergo a kind of rebirthing process. Palmer notes, "We are disabused of original giftedness in the first half of our lives. Then—if we are awake, aware, and able to admit our loss—we spend the second half trying to recover and reclaim the gift we once possessed."[11] He recalls his own process—how he wore other people's faces in the first half of his life; how in high school he spoke with the certitude that could be expected of that generation; how he wanted to be a navy aviator, and afterward to begin a career in advertising.

Interestingly, Palmer discovered that there was more to his boyhood fantasy. Over forty years later, he looks back at his seemingly radical departure from those early career dreams to becoming a Quaker, a would-be pacifist, a writer, and an activist. Taken literally, his original career ambitions illustrate how, early in life, one can lose track of who one is. "But," he writes, "inspected through the lens of paradox, my desire to become an aviator and an advertiser contain[s] clues to the core of true self that would take many years to emerge: clues, by definition, are coded and must be deciphered."[12]

---

9. Palmer, *Let Your Life Speak*, 2.
10. Palmer, *Let Your Life Speak*, 3.
11. Palmer, *Let Your Life Speak*, 12.
12. Palmer, *Let Your Life Speak*, 13.

What Palmer uncovered in his hidden desire to work in advertising was a need to channel his gift for creating powerful imagery through words. He also found that hidden within his dream to become a naval aviator lay something more complex, "a personal engagement with the problem of violence that expressed itself at first in military fantasies and then, over a period of years, resolved itself in the pacifism I aspire to today. When I flip the coin of identity I held to so tightly in high school, I find the paradoxical 'opposite' that emerged as the years went by."[13]

I have found the same to be true about teachers' early cues to their vocation. Most enacted their teaching roles through play, while others first entered jobs that required teaching skills, although "teaching" was not explicitly named as a qualification in the job description. I fit into both categories, having played at being a teacher, but then entering a different kind of teaching job. For example, my work in media required teaching clients about the medium I represented, and how using it as an advertising vehicle would match their goals. Adding to the similarity is that like in a classroom, my client presentations were sometimes done before large groups. The clues to my vocation were always quite clear, but although Palmer's seemed opposite to what he ultimately did with his life, the clues to his were there all along. He just needed to go further back in his life to see them.

As a young boy, Palmer dedicated much of his playtime to flying model airplanes. But, unlike many boys, he also spent countless hours drawing airplane and flight diagrams, writing explanatory captions, stapling everything onto pages, binding the pages, and painstakingly illustrating a cover. He recalls,

> I had always thought that the meaning of this paperwork was obvious: fascinated with flight, I wanted to be a pilot . . . But recently, when I found a couple of these literary artifacts in an old cardboard box, I suddenly saw the truth, and it was more obvious than I had imagined. I didn't want to be a pilot . . . or anything else related to aviation. I wanted to be an author, to make books—a task I have been attempting from the third grade to this very moment.[14]

His books, of course, became his tools for illuminating his passion—teaching. Drawing from his own experience, Palmer teaches that from the beginning, our interests are clues to our true identity. Sometimes, though, clues are difficult to decipher. He finds the process of decoding early clues to be

13. Palmer, *Let Your Life Speak*, 14.
14. Palmer, *Let Your Life Speak*, 15.

extremely meaningful and profoundly worthwhile, especially in adulthood, when we may have been pulled far away from our birthright gifts. He notes, "Those clues are helpful in counteracting the conventional concept of vocation, which insists that our lives must be driven by 'oughts.' . . . The deepest vocational question is not 'What ought I to do with my life?' It is the more elemental and demanding, 'Who am I? What is my nature?'"[15]

These two questions had a profound effect on me as I reviewed my own experiences. My biggest passion is to learn. For example, I come alive when I travel, which I do frequently. I came alive when I entered graduate school, and felt sad when it was time to graduate. It felt as though the intense learning experience and liveliness were coming to an end. I felt alive in the advertising world. In looking closer at these experiences, it is obvious that my learning experiences did not occur in a vacuum, that I was not thriving alone. I was deeply engaged with others, with the material, and with the world. I am social in nature, and thrive when I am in the right company. The emptiness that I have felt as a teacher speaks loudly to what I was missing; engagement with colleagues in a life-giving and meaningful way. This discovery not only freed me of the tyranny of feeling emotionally bankrupt at work, it drew my attention to what the experience must be like for those who have to live this way in general.

Palmer writes on a broader, more public scale about the social systems that oppress groups of people, forcing them to live in ways inauthentic to their nature. He notes,

> If you are poor, you are supposed to accept, with gratitude, half a loaf or less; if you are black, you are supposed to suffer racism without protest; if you are gay, you are supposed to pretend that you are not . . . [W]e can at least imagine, how tempting it would be to mask one's truth in situations of this sort—because the system threatens punishment if one does not.[16]

However, in spite of that threat, or because of it, there are people who make the critical decision to plant seeds of movements, deciding to live "divided no more."[17]

Palmer views Rosa Parks as emblematic of what the undivided life can mean. Her story begins with a seemingly innocent act: she sat down at the front of a bus in one of the seats reserved for whites. Palmer describes this

---

15. Palmer, *Let Your Life Speak*, 15.
16. Palmer, *Let Your Life Speak*, 32.
17. Palmer, *Let Your Life Speak*, 32.

moment as a dangerous, daring, and provocative act in a racist society."[18] He maintains, "Rosa Parks did not say that she sat down to launch a movement, because her motives were more elemental than that. She said, 'I sat down because I was tired.' But she did not mean that her feet were tired. She meant that her soul was tired, her heart was tired, her whole being was tired of playing by racist rules, of denying her soul's claim to selfhood."[19]

Palmer adds that Rosa Parks had many forces that shaped her decision to live authentically. Parks was a student of nonviolence theory and tactics at Highlander Folk School, where Martin Luther King Jr. also studied. She worked for the National Association for the Advancement of Colored People where, at the time, its members were discussing civil disobedience.[20] However, Palmer maintains that Parks's decision was especially courageous because she was acting upon a theory of nonviolence. She had no assurance that it would work, or that her community would embrace her actions. For Palmer, "It was a moment of existential truth, of claiming authentic selfhood, of reclaiming birthright giftedness—and in that moment she set in motion a process that changed both the lay and the law of the land."[21] He also views the moment as Rosa Parks embracing her true vocation, not only as someone who would change the status quo, but especially as a woman who became her true self in the world.

Palmer wondered, as do I, where people like Rosa Parks find the courage to live undividedly, especially in a world that often severely punishes anyone who deviates from what is socially acceptable. As in the example cited in the previous chapter, Palmer discovers answers when he reorders the words in the question that addresses the heart of the problem. He envisioned that instead of Rosa Parks asking: "What can I do to stop you from persecuting me?" she asked, "What can I do to stop myself from allowing this persecution?"

He argues that people like Rosa Parks "have transformed the notion of punishment itself." He affirms, "They have come to understand that no punishment anyone might inflict on them could possibly be worse than the punishment they inflict on themselves by conspiring in their own diminishment."[22] This reveals a dual meaning to the concept of conspiracy.

18. Palmer, *Let Your Life Speak*, 32.
19. Palmer, *Let Your Life Speak*, 33.
20. Palmer, *Let Your Life Speak*, 33.
21. Palmer, *Let Your Life Speak*, 33.
22. Palmer, *Let Your Life Speak*, 34.

Silence is a method of conspiring in the demise of someone else, but one can also "co-conspire" in one's own demise by remaining silent, albeit subconsciously. The actions of Rosa Parks helped to expose this truth to her people: that in their silence, they were allowing racist acts against them to continue.

For Palmer, when Rosa Parks refused to move to the back of the bus, she was making a statement: "What could your jail of stone and steel possibly mean to me, compared to the self-imposed imprisonment I've suffered for forty years—the prison I've just walked out of by refusing to conspire any longer with this racist system?"[23] However, he argues that if the story of Rosa Parks is to help individuals in any way, one should not look at her as a hero or icon of truth. She must be viewed as an ordinary person because when one looks at her in an exalted light, one tends to judge oneself as incapable of such bravery and thereby fall into the trap of perpetuating the conspiracy.

In a similar light, Palmer's own path toward honoring his true nature and needs was long, and sometimes painful. He recognized himself as a teacher at heart. However, the years he spent in higher education as a professor and community organizer were filled with restlessness and sometimes anger towards the institutions where he served. His teaching experience was marred by a love/hate relationship with the academy. He loved to teach but was disillusioned with the culture of the academy, which he described as tense, competitive, and lacking in authentic engagement between the students, the subject matter, and the professors.

Palmer yearned for community but spent his academic career in isolation. He wanted to resolve the incongruence that existed between how he felt and how he was in the world. Community organizing fulfilled this yearning, but the sense of fulfillment was short-lived because he did not feel authentic in these roles. He discovered that as an organizer, he was "trying to take people to places he had never been himself—a place called community."[24] He was clear that he needed much more life experience in community in order to do the work with authenticity. As a professor, the isolation he felt in the academy also impeded his ability to grow.

The search for community experience, which led to his years at Pendle Hill and later ventures, was part of Palmer's effort to close the gap between his inner and outer life. Paradoxically, it was long after he left the academy

---

23. Palmer, *Let Your Life Speak*, 34.
24. Palmer, *Let Your Life Speak*, 22.

out of frustration that his work came to focus on renewing educational institutions. He believes this happened because his true self forced him to find his rightful place in "the ecosystem of life."[25] He found "the right relation to institutions with which he had had a lifelong lover's quarrel."[26] He writes,

> Rosa Parks took her stand with clarity and courage. I took mine by diversion and default. Some journeys are direct, and some are circuitous; some are heroic, and some are fearful and muddled. But every journey, honestly undertaken, stands a chance of taking us toward the place where our deep gladness meets the world's deep need (Friedrich Buechner). The world needs people with the patience and the passion to make that pilgrimage not only for their sake but also as a social and political act.[27]

A divided life is a way of living that does not honor who the person truly is. As Palmer emphasizes, the path to an undivided life is through deep, inward listening to the wisdom of the spirit that dwells within us. The next section examines the path which led to his religious development.

PALMER'S RELIGIOUS DEVELOPMENT AND OUTLOOK: FORMATIVE INFLUENCES AND LATER CRITIQUE

In the foreword to *The Promise of Paradox*, Henri Nouwen offers insight into Palmer's religious life, saying:

> This book is important not because it is written by a good scholar, but because it is written by a scholar who dared to wonder if his scholarship really led him to truth . . . It is important not because it is written by a man who knows his Bible well, but because it is written by a man who dared to let the Bible make radical claims on his own life and the lives of those he loves.[28]

As Palmer came to know, especially through his years at Pendle Hill, the journey rightly taken allows us to find our true selves, and brings us back to caring for the needs of others. This resonates profoundly with religious

---

25. Palmer, *Let Your Life Speak*, 36.
26. Palmer, *Let Your Life Speak*, 35.
27. Palmer, *Let Your Life Speak*, 36.
28. Palmer, *Promise of Paradox*, 11.

concerns—the focus of the present chapter—and is significant for religious education, as will be addressed in the next chapter.

Palmer describes his religious development beginning with his journey as a child raised in the Methodist Church. At times, his choice of language in describing this early period appears to be anti-religious. For example, he uses words such as "distrust," "misguidance," and "misconceptions." Yet what he argues against represents specific negative aspects of his religious experience, not the totality of his views on the Methodist Church.

To begin, Palmer experienced a religious upbringing that was, and still is, typical for many Christians. The teachings that he appropriated were, and still are, very common in Christian communities. He had been raised a Methodist and described himself as a church-going person. He valued the Methodist tradition for its respect for humanity and efforts towards social justice. However, his experience of worship lacked spiritual depth. Going to church was a rote experience which consisted of hearing scriptural readings, listening to a homily, and singing a few hymns. Moments of intentional silence were not a part of the ritual.

It was in the Methodist Church that Palmer learned about vocation and ways of viewing life. Much of what he learned, however, were misconceptions that would hamper his approach to life and work. Years later, he relates that when he grew strong enough, he was able to discard the misinformed ideas for healthier ones. For example, one of the ideas he learned "was rooted in a deep distrust of selfhood, in the belief that the sinful self will always be 'selfish' unless corrected by external forces of virtue."[29] Another teaching that he assimilated was that "vocation, or calling, comes from a voice external to ourselves, a voice of moral demand that asks us to become someone we are not yet—someone different, someone better, someone just beyond our reach."[30]

After bearing the wounds of what he calls misguidance, in his adult years Palmer arrived at a new understanding of the self. He writes,

> By surviving passages of doubt and depression on the vocational journey, I have become clear about at least one thing: self-care is never a selfish act—it is simply good stewardship of the only gift I have, the gift I was put on earth to offer to others. Anytime we can

---

29. Palmer, *Let Your Life Speak*, 10.
30. Palmer, *Let Your Life Speak*, 10.

listen to our true self and give it the care it requires, we do so not only for ourselves but for the many others whose lives we touch.[31]

Palmer's ideas of becoming a pilot and an advertising executive are examples of looking outwardly for guidance as opposed to listening to his inner teacher. It is seemingly a natural tendency for most individuals to look to those they admire for clues to their own vocation. However, Palmer is warning against denying one's true self and engaging instead in the process of discernment that will lead to finding one's own vocation rather than the unauthenticity of seeking to imitate someone else's.

Morality seemed to be the touchstone of his religious beliefs as formed in his church, but rather than a message of happiness and hope, it served as a constant reminder of his and everyone's sinfulness. He notes, "the God I was told about in church, and still hear about from time to time, runs about like an anxious schoolmaster measuring people's behavior with a moral yardstick."[32] But in later years, the God that Palmer came to know "is the source of what *is* rather than what *ought* to be."[33] He adds that morality and the consequences of committing immoral acts are built into the God-given structure of reality itself. This also means that recognizing and honoring one's own limits as well as potentials "is a profoundly moral regimen."[34]

Much of what he learned about his sense of self is deeply imbued with the Hebrew Scriptures. This is evident in passages he quotes that speak to the nature of humans as created in the image of the God who, when asked by Moses for a name, responded: "I am who I am" (Exod 3:14). As Palmer remarks, "If, as I believe, we are all made in God's image, we could all give the same answer when asked who we are: 'I Am who I Am.' One dwells with God by being faithful to one's nature. One crosses God by trying to be something one is not. Reality—including one's own—is divine, to be not defied but honored."[35]

Palmer writes that as was typical for a white, middle-class American male, he was raised to believe that anything and everything was attainable for him, as long as he was willing to make the effort. This became the American dream for all of us, myself included: the ideal to which most people aspire and which they believe they can achieve regardless of gender,

31. Palmer, *Let Your Life Speak*, 30–31.
32. Palmer, *Let Your Life Speak*, 50.
33. Palmer, *Let Your Life Speak*, 50.
34. Palmer, *Let Your Life Speak*, 50.
35. Palmer, *Let Your Life Speak*, 51.

race, culture, or religion. This American dream ideology is somewhat like a religion. Gabriel Moran explains that the word "America" began as a "religious" term in 1507 and has continued to have religious connotations. America was to be the place of hope, promise, and fulfillment of those dreams. He writes, "America was Europe's name for the promised land out in the Western sea. America was another name for the Kingdom of God on earth."[36] Then, says Moran, the message became a cultural one—a distortion of the biblical message, but nevertheless with roots in the church.

As Palmer asserts, the American dream message can be harmful and misleading. It skews reality because it does not recognize limitations, including the systemic reality that for many people dreams do not come true, no matter how hard one works. I can speak to this truth as a Hispanic woman. I witnessed how hard both my parents struggled in life to give their children a better life and to secure their future. They persevered in their dream only to succumb to illness and die penniless. It was a very painful reality.

Palmer recalls the distorted reality under which he lived: "The message was that both the universe and I were without limits, given enough energy and commitment on my part. God made things that way, and all I had to do was to get with the program."[37] Another distorted reality that Palmer experienced was in his early religious formation. He had "embraced a form of Christian faith" that was not "devoted to the experience of God." It was steeped in ambiguities in which God was portrayed as a distant being almost removed from his own creation. He wonders, "How did so many disembodied concepts emerge from a tradition whose central commitment is to 'the Word become flesh'?"[38] As is evident from what came next, this was the missing element in his life: the experience of God. He describes his depression as "a total eclipse of light and hope."[39] It would take him years to absorb the meaning of the experience, and to see it as a pivotal passage on his pilgrimage toward selfhood and vocation.

To be clear, Palmer recommends the experience of deep depression to no one. He adds, "and I don't have to, for it arrives unbidden in too many lives."[40] For him, however, the experience led to the profound grace of find-

---

36. Moran, *Religious Education*, 16.
37. Palmer, *Let Your Life Speak*, 39.
38. Palmer, *Let Your Life Speak*, 67.
39. Palmer, *Let Your Life Speak*, 56.
40. Palmer, *Let Your Life Speak*, 57.

ing God. During his darkest moment, when he found the inner strength to ask himself, "What do you want?" the answer was clear:

> I want you to embrace this descent into hell as a journey toward selfhood—and a journey toward God. I had always imagined God to be in the same general direction as everything else that I valued: up. I had failed to appreciate the meaning of some words that had intrigued me since I first heard them in seminary—Tillich's description of God as the "ground of being." I had to be forced underground before I could understand that the way to God is not up but down.[41]

In retrospect, Palmer claims that what was missing during his church-going years was learning how to live religiously. He writes that "beliefs had simply been handed down to him or developed through reading and thinking."[42] Palmer does not refer to any positive influences of the Methodist tradition, which seems not to cohere with his earlier description of his family's formative influence during his youth. For example, in describing his father, he does not use the word "religious," but instead paints a portrait of a man who lived a life deeply committed to the values of his faith in his work, home, and in the world. In other words, Max Palmer knew how to live "religiously" and modeled this for his son. Palmer demonstrates this in speaking of his father with a sense of pride that came from the strong moral values that he had instilled in him as a child and as a young man. Among them were the belief that one's work should be done first and foremost with kindness, generosity, and integrity. Good will, not financial gain, was Max Palmer's principal goal.[43]

Clearly, these are good Christian beliefs and values that were conserved and passed down within the Palmer family. In fact, the values espoused by Max Palmer and handed down to his son can be equated to Horace Bushnell's (1847) model of Christian nurture. In raising a child to be Christian, Bushnell advocates for teaching the child a feeling of the divine, rather than a doctrine, and for teaching in a way that stimulates growth. He also emphasizes the centrality of home life for Christian nurture.[44] Max Palmer lived a life of faith in a way that demonstrated a divine

---

41. Palmer, *Let Your Life Speak*, 69–70.
42. Palmer, "Great People to Be Gathered," 4.
43. Intrator, *Living the Questions*, xxv, xxvii.
44. Boys, *Educating in Faith*, 40–42.

energy that lived within him. In turn, as Palmer affirms, he had a profound impact on his son's life and views.

Another question concerns Palmer's claim that he had not been "taught" to live his faith. In this statement, Palmer seems to miss an important element of what it means "to teach" or to be taught. Gabriel Moran best describes the meaning, writing that

> Most teaching is nonverbal; this fact is especially true of the moral and/or religious life . . . it does not seem an exaggeration to say that *most* teaching is not teaching of words but a teaching of activities in which speech is subordinate . . . A community life always involves speech [of various kinds] . . . However, none can substitute for religious and/or moral activity that is often in the form of a silent witness.[45]

For Palmer, simply being in his father's presence was life-giving, for there was a spirit about him that evidently brought out the best in his son. In reading about Palmer's relationship with his father, and his own life story, I developed the impression that father and son shared the same kind of energy, a spirituality that drove them both toward living a life of truth. The father did, indeed, teach his son how to live religiously and the son did, in fact, learn from him, perhaps not with words, but certainly through his silent witness.

An interest in community work forms another dimension of Palmer's religious convictions. Besides being a teacher at heart, he is an activist at heart, working to unite people for worthy causes, such as ameliorating racial tensions within diverse communities. This, coupled with his experiences at the intentional residential community of Pendle Hill, led him to discover a new perspective on the church. Pendle Hill gave him real-life experience about commitment to community. This led him to formulate a new theory of publicly-oriented religious commitment.

Animated by the meaning of the word "religion," which derives from Latin and means to bind together, Palmer began to view the possibilities for movement and change on a broad scale among people who are bound together by their religious affiliations. He began to understand the power of community in ways he had not previously imagined: the power of a spiritual and religious community organically formed within churches, orienting them toward both personal and social transformation.

---

45. Moran, *Religious Education*, 80–81.

As Palmer's thought developed, he formulated an expansive understanding of the nature and importance of communities of faith. First, the rich tradition of the Quakers at Pendle Hill, with their cohesive way of being and working together, gave him a new way of looking at communities of faith. Second, as he grew in his understanding about other religious communities, he came to think of synagogues as being part of faith communities in the broadest understanding of the term; a place to gather for worship, study, and prayer. In his 1981 book, *The Company of Strangers: Christians and the Renewal of America's Public Life*, Palmer claimed that there is no other institution that has the potential that the church and other faith communities have to heal the divide in our world. He wrote: "The church's potential for such a ministry can be indicated by a simple factual observation: the church is the largest and most diverse voluntary association in America today."[46] A current study by the Pew Research Center (2021) shows that the number of religiously unaffiliated Americans has grown to 22.8 percent with trends continuing to be more pronounced among young adults. However, the religiously affiliated (76.5 percent) remain a sizeable number, which still supports Palmer's idea of the community within the church as a source of power.[47]

Another critical element of the church, according to Palmer, is that it is not only large, but diverse. Its members span races, economic levels, and political orientations. He believes that this puts the church in the unique position to bridge the private and the public realms, and help people walk across the gap. Since the church is grounded in healing the divide between people, it gives its members a sense of solidarity. As he notes, "the church is engaged in a relentless divine calling to engage in the work of reconciliation—to God, to one another, and to ourselves."[48]

The Christian message of healing the divide within individuals and society undergirds Palmer's work. However, nearly three decades after writing *The Company of Strangers*, he found that the attitude of the church, which still tends to distance communities of faith from the broader world rather than immersing them in it, required that he take a new approach. Specifically, Palmer began to reflect upon the language he was using, and recognized that there was a problem, another paradox. He realized that using Christian language was ineffective in motivating people to work towards

---

46. Palmer, *Company of Strangers*, 27.
47. Pew Research Center, "Measuring Religion."
48. Palmer, *Company of Strangers*, 26–28.

healing the divide. Too many Christians, despite maintaining their identity as religiously affiliated, had lost faith in the church and were turning away from it, which explained the rise in unaffiliated which is at 22.8 percent, as documented in the 2021 Pew Research report. It was also obvious that, by his choice of language, he was reaching a smaller audience than might be possible. Paradoxically, it became necessary for him to avoid religious language in order to convey his message of hope.

When he reissued *The Promise of Paradox: A Celebration of Contradictions in the Christian Life* in 2008, he stated in the introduction, "I still understand myself as a Christian, and many traditional Christian understandings still shape my life. But . . . traditional Christian language . . . has been taken hostage by theological terrorists and tortured beyond recognition. Of course, this is not the first time Christian rhetoric has been violated in public places."[49] Palmer also criticized the exclusivist attitude that is prevalent in the church: an arrogant claim that salvation is only available through Christianity, and that all outsiders are doomed to eternal damnation. He wonders: "How can it be that Christianity—named after one who proclaimed that 'the meek shall inherit the earth'—can give rise to so much arrogance?"[50]

Thus, while *The Promise of Paradox* and *The Company of Strangers* are both steeped in Christian language, Palmer's later works tend more towards secular language. He intentionally refrains from using the word "God" and makes no mention of Jesus. In the revised introduction for *The Promise of Paradox,* he states that he has "worked hard to find a language about the inner life that builds bridges, not walls, and today I am grateful to have readers who are Christians and non-Christians."[51] The feedback he has received from his diverse readership confirms that he has succeeded in this regard.

While Palmer indeed draws a large audience through secular language, his work is nevertheless steeped in the wisdom of ancient religious traditions of the East as well as the West, giving his message broader appeal. For example, threads of the Taoist concept of Yin and Yang holding two opposites together shape Palmer's understanding of paradoxes.[52] Many of his books contain the teachings and poetry of Taoist master Chuang Tzu. Another example is the Noble Truths of Buddhism, one of which teaches

---

49. Palmer, *Promise of Paradox*, xxi.
50. Palmer, *Promise of Paradox*, xxii.
51. Palmer, *Promise of Paradox*, xiv.
52. Wong, *Taoism*, 18.

that suffering is caused by wanting things to be as they are not, a concept which Palmer draws from in his theory of a divided life.[53] A parallel can also be drawn with the basic principles of Jainism: non-violence, non-attachment, and non-absolutism, concepts which Palmer strongly advocates as a teacher and community organizer.[54] In his integration of Eastern spirituality Merton's influence is clearly apparent. Palmer notes that Merton enjoyed exploring the "other side of things," and although other spiritual practices seemed contradictory to Christianity, Merton showed how the very contradictions "open into deeper truth."[55]

Palmer's own curiosity about the other side of things would attract an audience that hungered for his message and bring him an unanticipated level of recognition. In the process, he also developed spiritually and broadened his outlook about himself and the world around him.

PALMER'S SPIRITUAL DEVELOPMENT AND THE IMPACT OF PENDLE HILL

Palmer's spiritual development was triggered by the unrest he experienced in his life. Viewed through Rolheiser's definition, Palmer's unrest, his tendency to search inwardly, his love of truth and knowledge-seeking mind, is his signature—his spirituality. As I mentioned in the previous chapter, two events played a pivotal role in his spiritual development in his early to middle adult years: his decision to move to Pendle Hill, and the work of Thomas Merton.

At Pendle Hill, Palmer experienced the paradoxes of life. He learned that to become fully engaged in fellowship, demands solitude; that when you create an extended family, it is necessary to draw firm boundaries around your own; and that when you are determined to elude the world around you, you will find yourself more connected and more grounded in the world than ever before.

In contrast to communal life, Palmer concluded that the privacy found in suburban life is the commodity of the rich. Buying expensive cars, household help, and vacationing around the world only serves to distance us from one another, because in doing so, we can "deny the underlying truth of our interdependence." The truth, he felt, is that "independence is

---

53. Keown, *Buddhism*, 51.
54. Jain, *Faith and Philosophy*, 38.
55. Palmer, *Promise of Paradox*, 8.

an unnatural condition for the human species, so just beneath the surface of our privileged privatism lies a cavern of loneliness."[56]

To understand the complexities of human needs and desires, Palmer analyzed a person's development from infancy, or stage one, through adulthood. He sought to articulate how it is that we are born with the birthright gift of self and how it is then lost. He reasoned that a constructed self-image dichotomized between "outer" and "inner" life begins to happen at stage two, which is school age, and the time at which the child goes out into the world alone and begins to feel vulnerable in the world, confronted with challenges about personal values and truths. People soon learn to deal with peer pressure by hiding their truth. Sometimes, they hide their true nature to the extent that they ultimately lose sight of who they truly are.

As a person matures, they may reach a third phase in which they seek to merge their onstage and backstage lives into a healthy balance, by centering around core, backstage beliefs and values. Ideally, what people are yearning for in this phase is to have their inner truth guide the choices they make in their lives and how they conduct themselves in the world. It is a yearning to be centered on inner truth. However, as Palmer has noted, this phase has a "shadow side." It could draw a person to exclude everyone and everything that they do not find agreeable.[57] Palmer explains that when individuals interpret "truth" in this insular way, they are in direct opposition to what the great spiritual traditions stand for. He suggests that the two sides of people's lives must exist in relation to one another.[58]

It seems that the catalyst for the spiritual development of Palmer's inner and outer life was his experience at Pendle Hill. This is where stillness and compassion surrounded him. This, along with his studies and everyday community experiences gave him the time and tools necessary to rebuild his theology into a practiced theology, "from the ground of his own being."[59] One of the spiritual lessons he learned was that:

> Community is that place where the person you least want to live with always lives, and when that person moves away, someone else arrives immediately to take his or her place. What I am referring to, of course, is the fact that in the closeness and intenseness of community there is always someone on whom to project

---

56. Palmer, *Promise of Paradox*, 58.
57. Palmer, *Hidden Wholeness*, 46.
58. Palmer, *Hidden Wholeness*, 47.
59. Palmer, "Great People to Be Gathered," 304.

that which you cannot abide in yourself. One of the great gifts of community is the chance to see yourself in the mirror of another person, and by forgiving that person, to forgive yourself as well.[60]

Also discussed in the previous chapter and relevant for Palmer's spirituality is his interest in poetry. Meaningful revelations come to us when we become aware that in discerning the meaning of a poem, we are saying things about ourselves. Whether we are drawn to or repelled by the story or someone's interpretation of it, we are often projecting our own inner issues. If we try to understand our own response, we may discover that our inner teacher has something important to tell us.

In summary, it was at Pendle Hill that Palmer began to live the experiences that led to the development of his mature spiritual perspectives. It was also there that he came to grasp more fully the meaning behind the work of Thomas Merton.

THE SPIRITUAL INFLUENCE OF THOMAS MERTON

Thomas Merton was born in Prades, France, in 1915 and died in Bangkok, Thailand, in 1968. In 1947, Merton received consecration as a monk in the Cistercian Order, and became known by his monastic name, Father Louis. Merton was a profoundly spiritual man, a mystic, and a brilliant scholar.

Merton's most outstanding gift was his ability to write. He became a prolific writer. He was also a man of intense energy and vision. In examining the writings of Merton, it becomes clear that his influence on Palmer is considerable. The following pages highlight some of the themes that Palmer appropriated from studying Merton.

Having entered the monastery as an idealistic young man, Merton soon discovered that when you leave the world behind, you take yourself with you. Palmer encountered this reality when he entered Pendle Hill, and it forced him to examine and discover his true self. Self-examination was also important to Merton. The question of identity was a lifelong concern for him and prevalent throughout his writings. For example, when he entered the monastery, he recalled: "But then there was this shadow, this double, this writer who had followed me into the cloister."[61] Merton learned that in silence and solitude, he really had to face himself. He considered solitude

---

60. Palmer, "Great People to Be Gathered," 5.
61. Quoted in Bamberger, "Monk," 53.

to be a gift oriented to the recovery of one's deep self. Solitude had a deep existential meaning involving all people. He wrote, "If a man can't be alone, he doesn't know who he is."[62]

These concepts posed significant questions for Palmer. In examining his own life, he explored his shadow side. He adopted Merton's theory that self-knowledge was not exclusively about humans recognizing their potential, but about acknowledging their limitations as well. He later wrote that living with a strong sense of identity and integrity also means recognizing that "the self is not infinitely elastic."[63]

Another gift that Merton possessed was his ability to be himself. This is evident by the testimonies in the collection of essays written about him, and edited by his long-time secretary, Brother Patrick Hart. In one essay, Matthew Kelty remarks, "He was nothing if not real. And part of that reality was his simplicity, his being himself. He said what he thought and did what he thought should be done, and that was all there was to it. And what he said and what he did was rooted in love for God and man."[64] It was through Merton's writings that Palmer began to develop the concept of living an undivided life, the key to which was self-knowledge and self-acceptance. Merton wrote extensively about the importance of living an authentic, integrated life, and this theme became the cornerstone of Palmer's work.

According to his friends, Merton was also a man of many contradictions. Kelty notes that while he was an obedient monk, he also enjoyed the local pubs. He insisted that "if ascesis did not spring from within the man, it was of little use, and of no use if imposed."[65] John Eudes Bamberger recalls that in spite of his intense and unvarying attraction to solitude, he was one of the most sociable of men. David Steindl-Rast found him "at once so totally uninhibited and perfectly disciplined."[66] Merton lived contradictions and wrote extensively about paradox, a topic of great interest to Palmer.

Faith and doubt are one of the paradoxes upon which Merton expounded. He wrote: "You can't have faith without doubt. Give up the business of suppressing doubt. Doubt and faith are two sides of the same coin. Faith grows from doubt, the real doubt."[67] Animated by Merton's insights,

---

62. Lentfoehr, "Solitary," 78.
63. Palmer, *Let Your Life Speak*, 9.
64. Kelty, "Man," 28.
65. Kelty, "Man," 34.
66. Steindl-Rast, "Man of Prayer," 85.
67. Quoted in Steindl-Rast, "Man of Prayer," 89.

in 1980 Palmer wrote *The Promise of Paradox*, in which he explores paradoxes such as the cross of Jesus. He sheds new light on this depiction by explaining it as a symbol of the way humans are pulled, left and right, then up and down, between conflicting demands and obligations in life's vertical and horizontal planes.[68]

Merton, whose spiritual beliefs and practices are greatly influenced by Eastern traditions, believed that "life consists in learning to live one's own, spontaneous, freewheeling life: to do this one must recognize what is one's own—be familiar and at home with oneself. This means basically learning who one is, and learning what one has to offer to the contemporary world, and then learning how to make that offering valid."[69] Furthermore, as in the Buddhist teachings on meditation, Merton also had a reverence for stillness. He recognized that in silence lay the path to inner growth. He taught that in solitude and stillness, we will find that we already possess everything we need. He advocated developing and nurturing an "interior solitude, interiority that we can have in the midst of crowds and every distraction."[70]

Palmer's concept of the inner teacher developed from these thoughts. He wrote that we are accustomed to thinking that answers can be found through others. Rarely do we recognize our own power. The inner teacher reveals itself in stillness, solitude, and silence. It leads us toward that which we already possess, the answers we seek.[71]

Merton spoke out against commercialism and popular culture for their false and manipulative messages promising self-fulfillment. He was repelled by how many individuals are dominated by public opinion, which he felt contributed to the divisiveness that exists within each of us, the false self and the true self. Palmer developed his theory of the divided life, basing its cause on social pressures. Merton acknowledged that it takes much courage and insight to be your true self. And, like Palmer, he found wisdom in the teachings of Christian foremothers and forefathers as well as those of other religious traditions.

Merton wrote: "In Sufism, Zen Buddhism and in many other religious or spiritual traditions, emphasis is placed on the call to fulfill certain obscure yet urgent potentialities in the ground of one's being, to 'become someone' that one already (potentially) is, the person one is truly meant

---

68. Palmer, *Promise of Paradox*, 30.
69. Merton, *Love and Living*, 3.
70. Lentfoehr, "Solitary," 71.
71. Palmer, *Hidden Wholeness*, 54.

to be. Zen calls this awakening a recognition of 'your original face before you were born.'"[72] Palmer incorporated Zen and Sufism teachings into his theory of the undivided life, referring to what Merton calls the "true self" and our birthright gift.[73]

Community was also the thrust of many of Merton's writings. Toward the end of his life, he spoke openly and passionately to his fellow monks about the issues he saw amongst them that were impeding community in its true sense of the word. He spoke about what he saw as their "false theology." He states: "We are broken persons and live in broken communities in a state of brokenness. We are alienated from ourselves and from each other . . . If we want to be recollected, that is, centered and gathered in God, then let us drop all walls and be completely open. . . ."[74] Bamberger notes that he opposed anything that was inauthentic, "not only in personal relations but especially in the 'institutions.'"[75] Palmer was extremely sensitive to the divisiveness and brokenness in the academy, to the inauthentic ways in which people interacted with one another there. His life-long criticism of the institution mirrors the inauthentic way of life that Merton witnessed in the monastery.

Authenticity, interdependence, and solidarity are also the qualities of a social activist, a characteristic that Palmer shares with Merton. Merton emerged as one of the most effective social critics of the political and racial policies pursued by the United States government. Jean Leclercq writes, "Thomas Merton was the man Christianity needed in a time of transition which began, not with Vatican II, but with World War II. Earlier than others, he had seen, he had known without a doubt that—in monasticism as well as in everything else—many things would change."[76] Similarly, Palmer's book *Healing the Heart of Democracy*, delves into the issues of living an integrated life as citizens and public leaders. He writes, "The heart is where everything begins: that grounded place in each of us where we can overcome fear, rediscover that we are members of one another, and embrace the conflicts that threaten democracy."[77] Like Merton, Palmer has emerged as an effective social critic of U.S. policies.

72. Merton, "Final Integration," 201.
73. Palmer, *Let Your Life Speak*, 68.
74. Pennington, *Thomas Merton, My Brother*, 31.
75. Bamberger, "Monk," 46.
76. Leclerq, "Evolving Monk," 98.
77. Palmer, "Great People to Be Gathered."

In conclusion, the spiritual influence that Merton had on Palmer was largely due to the fact that these two individuals, though they never met, shared a thirst for self-knowledge and a vision for change. Studying the work of Merton introduced Palmer to a world that he seemed to have been unconsciously seeking for most of his life: an inner world that contained a hidden wholeness. Subsequently, it was Henri Nouwen who helped Palmer further his spiritual development. Nouwen taught by example, giving Palmer the courage to reveal his wounds openly. This was a pivotal step in Palmer's life towards living authentically.

THE SPIRITUAL INFLUENCE OF HENRI NOUWEN

Henri Nouwen was born in 1932 in Nijkerk, Netherlands. He died in his homeland in 1996. In 1957, he was ordained a Roman Catholic priest for the archdiocese of Utrecht, Holland. He shared many similarities with Thomas Merton. Like Merton, Nouwen was profoundly spiritual. His deepest aspiration was to emulate Jesus in his own life and ministry. He was also a prolific writer. By the end of his life, he had written over forty books, along with numerous essays and articles. He had also delivered a vast number of sermons and lectures throughout the United States and abroad. And, like Merton, his office and life were a frenetic whirlwind of activity.

He and Parker Palmer met in the mid-1970s when Nouwen was already a well-known and respected writer, having published his famous book, *The Wounded Healer*, in 1972. A lasting friendship emerged between them. They enjoyed a decade of shared work, collaborating on writings and other projects. And, although Nouwen was only seven years older, Palmer considered him his mentor and a spiritual virtuoso. In 1980, Nouwen wrote the Introduction to Palmer's book *The Promise of Paradox*. In his praise for Palmer's accomplishment, Nouwen acknowledges how much Palmer taught him over the years.

In reading Nouwen's work and comparing it to Palmer's, the stark similarities make it difficult to determine who influenced whom. In fact, Nouwen had already provided in his writings much of the groundwork that Palmer then built upon, namely, the theme of the wounded healer and the importance of community. Palmer himself tells us that the courage to write about his own depression developed from an invitation to honor the memory of Nouwen in writing on the theme of the wounded healer.[78] The

---

78. Palmer, *Let Your Life Speak*, 57.

following analysis outlines Nouwen's influence on Palmer, as well as the common ground they shared.

Nouwen's friends remember how "courageously he stood with one foot in the shadow of self-rejection and one foot in the daylight of God's love." Jonas reflects, "Many of us would have preferred that Henri's human woundedness be less visible. But somehow, we know that his ever-present, accompanying shadow was there only because of the Light in which he walked."[79] This characteristic was also a gift that Nouwen shared with Merton: his ability to be himself wherever he went. Nouwen himself suggested that "such inward, tender places can be a point of connection with all human beings, even those who seem very different from us. He ends his reflections, as always, with the message that 'somehow,' 'somewhere,' joy arises right here, in the midst of darkness."[80]

Palmer recognized that Nouwen's strength as a priest and teacher came from his willingness to be vulnerable. He understood it as an authentic part of Nouwen. He learned that revealing one's woundedness or expressing vulnerability can serve as a point of connection to one another. He also saw woundedness, as Nouwen did, as a way of healing others. Palmer adopted this as a central theme in his work about the undivided life.

It was through the pain of fear and isolation, and through living dividedly, that Palmer himself emerged as a wounded healer. Identity, integrity, authenticity, and vulnerability became themes in his theories about living an undivided life. Palmer explores these concepts at length and adapts them to education in *The Courage to Teach*, his most widely read book.

Jonas also notes that Nouwen was a master at identifying scriptural passages that promised joy amidst sorrow. According to Nouwen, "the story of the Prodigal Son was the center of gravity of Jewish and Christian Scripture, the heart of mystical teaching."[81] He believed that "the parable is somehow true for each one of us: even though we rebel, and reject our birthright, our God will always welcome us back, embracing us with unconditional love."[82] Palmer came to understand the richness of this gift years later when he was at the lowest point in his life, facing clinical depression.

---

79. Jonas, "Introduction," xiv.
80. Jonas, "Introduction," xxix.
81. Jonas, "Introduction," xv.
82. Jonas, "Introduction," xv.

He wrote, "I heard a voice say, simply and clearly, 'I love you, Parker' . . . It was a moment of inexplicable grace."[83]

Nouwen also revealed mystical qualities in his role as priest and teacher, an authentic manifestation of his gift. What he said was important, but even more fundamental for some was who he was as he said it. Friends report that he underwent a transformation during his lectures and while celebrating Mass. Witnesses saw him "in the exhilaration of an ecstatic vision that became more and more vivid to him, and to us, as he declared its reality."[84] Palmer recognized the depth of Nouwen's spirituality and held him in the highest regard.

Palmer writes that during their years together, although Nouwen shared his darkest side with him, Palmer was too ashamed to reveal his own longtime struggle with depression. It took years, and Nouwen's influence, for Palmer to come to terms publicly with his own demons.[85] To some, it would seem ironic that this was when Palmer became most successful in life. However, it was actually living proof of his own theory about how one's life could change when one summons the courage and decides to live an undivided, authentic life.

Harvard, Yale, and Notre Dame were three principal institutions where Nouwen taught. He valued intellectual thought and critique. But he also valued the knowledge that comes from the soul, which takes us to higher levels of understanding. Because his interests tended more toward people than theological scholarship, he studied and taught psychology, connecting the insights of modern psychology with spiritual practice and understanding. Palmer shares this interest in psychology. Much of his work is about how socialization leads one far away from one's true self.

Nouwen believed that ministers should remain grounded in their own vulnerability. He viewed ministry as living the life of Jesus, making oneself available in body and spirit to minister. In *The Wounded Healer*, he writes, "no minister can save anyone. He can only offer himself as a guide to fearful people. Yet, paradoxically, it is precisely in this guidance that the first signs of hope become visible. This is so because a shared pain is no longer paralyzing but mobilizing, when understood as a way to liberation."[86] Palmer

---

83. Palmer, *Let Your Life Speak*, 65.
84. Jonas, "Introduction," xviii.
85. Palmer, *Let Your Life Speak*, 57.
86. Nouwen, *Wounded Healer*, 93.

later wrote about the importance of the teacher being present and available to the students as a whole person, revealing strengths as well as weaknesses.

Nouwen wrote, "making one's own wounds a source of healing . . . calls for a constant willingness to see one's own pain and suffering as rising from the depth of the human condition which all [humans] share."[87] For example, he found that loneliness is an important aspect of this human condition, and experienced loneliness in his professional life. He describes the life of the minister as one who stands at the margins of all activity, waiting to be summoned mostly when there is pain and suffering. The minister, he wrote, "always seems to arrive at the wrong places at the wrong times with the wrong people, outside the walls of the city when the feast is over, with a few crying women."[88] The pain of loneliness that he felt in his career became all the more piercing as he observed that the role of ministers began to have a diminishing impact on others.[89]

After leaving Harvard in 1985, Nouwen experienced many intense changes. He struggled with intimacy, his academic career, depression, and a near fatal accident in the late 1980s.[90] However, in his hard work of spiritual discipline, Nouwen discovered the "promise of paradox," a phrase that he originally used in his writings and which Palmer eventually adopted. He learned that power can emerge from weakness, as in his ability to heal others because of his own woundedness. He learned that light is the promise in darkness, as in the possibility of coming out of a sickness even stronger than before. He also learned that resurrection is the promise in death, in that death is not finite, as new life awaits after death. In all of Nouwen's books, the prevalent theme is of humbly returning to the ground of who and what we actually are. In 2000, Palmer based his work on this theme of paradox in Nouwen's work. He wrote about his depression and finding God, calling it a journey to the underground: a journey to God as the ground of being.

Another topic that was of great interest to Nouwen was the idea of fear. He believed that all thoughts spring from fear. He wrote: "we are afraid of the violence in our streets and homes; we are afraid of what people think of us; we are afraid of failure, of intimacy, of God; and we are even afraid of ourselves and our desires."[91] Palmer expanded on this concept of fear and

---

87. Nouwen, *Wounded Healer*, 88.
88. Nouwen, *Wounded Healer*, 86.
89. Nouwen, *Wounded Healer*, 86.
90. Jonas, "Introduction," xviii.
91. Jonas, "Introduction," xlviii.

applied it to teaching. He developed the framework for his book, *The Courage to Teach*, based on the obstacles that fear represents. Nouwen spoke of fear as a general condition, the human condition. For Nouwen, fear affected nearly every aspect of human life. This insight resonates with many people, and is likely one of the reasons why Palmer's book is so widely read.

Yet despite all these similarities, there was one significant area in which Palmer and Nouwen differed, and that was in their response to their dissatisfaction with institutional life. At Harvard Divinity School, Nouwen perceived a complete lack of community, and a valuing of competition over prayer.[92] Jonas recalls:

> Although Henri always preached a vision of social and economic justice, he simultaneously tried not to criticize people or institutions . . . In almost all situations of actual or potential conflict, he avoided direct confrontation, focusing instead on the positive, motivating vision of the Good News.[93]

In contrast, Palmer was very public about his dissatisfaction with academic life. Much of what he wrote in *The Courage to Teach,* and in numerous articles, included criticism of the competitiveness and isolation within the academy.

Despite this difference, there were far more substantive things that the two shared, especially their woundedness. Palmer learned that by revealing his weakness and vulnerability he would "give his readers permission to claim their own 'shadow side' and to see that Christ is present even there—and, perhaps, especially there."[94] As Palmer acknowledges, Nouwen was the one who gave him the courage to share his wounds as well. He notes that it was a wonderful gift from a friend who left this world much too soon.[95] Nouwen taught him about the depth of healing that one's wounds can provide. He also helped Palmer to find his voice and to share it with a world in need of hearing it.

---

92. Jonas, "Introduction," xlix.
93. Jonas, "Introduction," xli.
94. Jonas, "Introduction," lxvi.
95. Palmer, *Let Your Life Speak*, 57.

CONCLUDING THOUGHTS

Though many people and life experiences shaped him, Parker J. Palmer's religious and spiritual development was most heavily influenced by Thomas Merton, Henri Nouwen, and his experiences at Pendle Hill. These particular encounters are the cornerstone of how spirituality, living authentically, and the importance of community developed as elements undergirding and permeating Palmer's theory of education. The next chapter explores this aspect of his life and work.

Chapter 3

THE SPIRITUALITY OF TEACHING

Nearly a century ago, John Dewey was asked his opinion of IQ tests. He responded with the following story of "his family's preparations for taking a hog to market":

> In order to figure out how much to charge for the animal, his family put the hog on one end of a seesaw and piled bricks on the other until the two balanced. Then we tried to figure out how much those bricks weighed, said Dewey.[1]

Parker J. Palmer, a firm believer in the power of story-telling, offers this tale to make a point about one of the major problems he finds with the U.S. educational system. He equates the bricks in this story to the many "measures of learning" developed over time, and to our continuing obsession with educational externals.[2] He notes, "Today we say, in effect, 'This child weighs seventy-six bricks worth of language skills, while that one weighs eighty-three bricks.' But we still don't know how much the bricks weigh—and the kinds of bricks we use differ from one setting to another!"[3]

These statements refer to the many different methods used today to measure a student's intellectual ability. One example is the required national standardized tests administered in public schools to measure a student's aptitude across various subjects. However, private schools have no such requirement and use their own forms of assessment. In addition to the various methodologies employed, Palmer is also critical of what it is that schools purport to be measuring.

1. Palmer, *Courage to Teach*, xiii.
2. Palmer, *Courage to Teach*, xiii.
3. Palmer, *Courage to Teach*, xiv.

Moran writes that the problem in education is the dearth of literature about teaching, specifically about how to teach. It begs the question: Why is so little written about such an important profession? He contends, "Nearly all books on teaching leave out the main story. Most often, they do not even raise the question of the meaning of 'to teach' . . . My thesis is that people are uneasy with the very idea of teaching. By 'people' I mean a good part of the general population, including people who write books on education."[4]

My own experiences as a teacher confirm these findings. I do not believe that I have ever come across a teacher (myself included) who, after completing coursework in education, could claim that they had learned anything about teaching. Most of what I learned in coursework were theories about teaching, and my teaching experience in a classroom was more about observing than about actual teaching. There seems to be an underlying assumption that one is ready to teach as long as one has completed the degree. As a result, once one begins to work as a teacher, the initial classroom experience is generally very intimidating. Adding to the feeling of intimidation is that the classroom experience does not seem to get easier with time, at least not for a very long time. Most beginner teachers, meaning those who have been teaching for a couple of years, tell me that they try to figure out what to do in the classroom as they go along. In other words, learning about teaching occurs by trial and error, and oftentimes guesswork.

Elizabeth Green supports this viewpoint. The central suggestion of her 2015 book, *Building A+ Better Teacher: How Teaching Works,* is that teachers would benefit from actively sharing their classroom experiences so as to continually teach one another about the art of teaching. It's a concept that runs counter to the isolation that Palmer vehemently criticized about the academy. Green focuses on the theories developed by Francis Parker, who taught in the mid-1800s, because they are still relevant today. Parker believed that teaching well required intense study but also, most importantly, practice. He viewed good teaching as a craft, an art which could take a lifetime to achieve.[5]

Furthermore, central to Parker's theory is his conviction that in order to learn how to teach, one must have access to the knowledge that experienced teachers have acquired. Green writes that unfortunately, Parker was practically alone in his thinking. The general public did not view teaching

---

4. Moran, *Showing How*, 1.
5. Green, *Building A+ Better Teacher*, 19.

as a craft or a discipline that required study. Nonetheless, Parker helped to develop a school for teachers in Chicago which was based on his principles. However, he died before seeing his dream become a reality.[6] Later, philosopher John Dewey, who was Parker's successor at the University of Chicago, wrote about the "science of education," which he hoped to develop into a practical theory but was not well received. His vision was to "prevent the immeasurable waste that comes from letting great teachers' secrets die with them."[7]

However, although Parker and Dewey died, their vision did not. Entrepreneurial educators with promising dreams have emerged to implement it, and Green writes about the work of some of them, including Magdalene Lampert and Deborah Ball, two visionaries who in the 1980s collaborated on a pioneer program on the "wisdom of practice" at Michigan State's *Institute for Research on Teaching*.[8] The two were not only researchers but also elementary school mathematics teachers who were eager to share their discoveries about better ways to help students learn. Lambert and Ball became living proof that one can teach differently and reach students at a deeper level.[9] Nonetheless, these visionaries still constitute a minority in this country.

The theories of teaching and learning that form Palmer's philosophy of education are the subject of this chapter. However, of primary importance is his understanding of the spirituality of the teacher. This undergirds his theory of education, and is, perhaps, his most significant contribution to the field of education. As such, it will be explored first. Thereafter, the chapter presents how Palmer envisions a transformational pedagogy by examining his understanding of the nature of knowledge, and how this understanding forms the basis for his re-imaging of education.

Key to his perspective is his position against the Western mode of knowing: objective, analytic, and experimental. Palmer follows Thomas Merton in characterizing such ways of knowing as not only limiting human potential but lending themselves to "subtle, but pervasive forms of violence to our personal and social lives."[10] This argument delves into the outcome of a limited understanding about teaching that results, coupled with the

6. Green, *Building A+ Better Teacher*, 20.
7. Green, *Building A+ Better Teacher*, 20.
8. Green, *Building A+ Better Teacher*, 67.
9. Green, *Building A+ Better Teacher*, 316.
10. Palmer, "Violence of Our Knowledge," 3.

impersonal, detached approach to examining a subject. In the context of Palmer as the wounded healer, this chapter examines this experience-based claim in relation to the alternative approach he advocates.

The chapter also explores his ideas about re-imagining education in ways that involve teaching to the totality of the person by tapping into the various human senses. Of particular significance is his practical application of connected, engaged, and imaginative forms of teaching. The chapter examines these ideas, and concludes with his theory of transformational pedagogy.

THE INNER SPIRITUALITY OF THE TEACHER

Palmer argues that, because of the obsession with externals in education, which include curriculum, grades, techniques, etc., we overlook the primary resource—the teacher. His concern is not only for the person known as teacher, but also for the inner life of the teacher. As such, his theory of education is deeply spiritual and profoundly humanistic. He maintains, "We teach who we are."[11] This means that one's personality traits, one's likes and dislikes, and one's worries and concerns are all revealed in the way one does one's work. In his words, "the personal can never be divorced from the professional."[12] Palmer came to this realization when, after three decades of teaching, he still had moments when his classes went as poorly as when he was a novice. Disheartened by his failures, and perplexed by the mystery of his chosen vocation, he began to ponder the question: "Who is the self that teaches?"[13] Efforts to answer this question became one of the hallmarks of his career.

In the process of exploring the profession of school teaching, Palmer uncovered many factors that can cause a teacher to feel defeated and become disheartened and disillusioned. He drew attention to the fact that when problems arise in the classroom or in the system, it is automatically assumed that the teachers are at fault. The accusations are waged from all angles: politicians, the media, parents, and school administrators. In many cases he notes that teachers are neglected, and in others, diminished as a person.

---

11. Palmer, *Courage to Teach*, xi.
12. Palmer, *Courage to Teach*, xi.
13. Palmer, *Courage to Teach*, 4.

My own experience and observation in various school settings confirms this assertion. The needs of the teacher are often met with dismissive attitudes. This attitude seems to be ingrained in the general school culture. I sensed early on that teachers were viewed as servants to their students, always stepping back into the shadows of the students, and stepping forward when beckoned. Adding to the sense of diminishment is the fact that there is no finite list that delineates the specific tasks that teachers are expected to complete each day. Given this, the expectations of school administrators are limitless, which includes invading your personal time.

Teaching during a pandemic is an excellent example of stretching teachers beyond their limits. Literally overnight, teachers had to learn how to teach a classroom of students without anyone's physical presence. Managing a virtual classroom of students led to extreme fatigue, and an unwavering sense among the teachers that we were being exploited. When students were allowed back in the school building, the conditions became even worse. We then had to navigate teaching half the students in the class, while half were at home or in some other part of the school building. To add to the tyranny, we did all of this while wearing a mask all day to protect ourselves. During that period, schools boasted about how much more their teachers were doing for their students, in comparison to other schools. The servant role of teachers, which some might argue at times is more of a slave role, became a selling point to parents.

Palmer addresses the overall issues that teachers face. He writes, "We blame teachers for being unable to cure social ills that no one knows how to treat. Teachers are held responsible for adopting whatever 'solution' has most recently been concocted by our national panacea machine, and in the process, we demoralize, even paralyze the very teacher who could help us find our way."[14] The various protests held each year by teachers throughout the country can be viewed as expressing these concerns, as well as responding to specific issues such as the poor compensation that teachers receive for such unrealistic expectations.

In addition, the pressure to conform to the latest trend diminishes the teacher's voice, sending a message that their method of teaching is substandard and that external forces will dictate what happens in the classroom. He adds that unlike many other professions, teachers are susceptible to public scorn, ridicule, and offensive remarks from students, and maintains that a public backlash is rare in other professions. He explains that, for example, a

---

14. Palmer, *Courage to Teach*, 4.

good therapist can only work privately. Simply disclosing a patient's identity is considered negligence. Trial lawyers work publicly, but can never allow their personal opinion or feelings to interfere with a case. Any trial lawyer who does this is guilty of malpractice.

However, in analyzing the teaching profession, Palmer finds that "As we try to uncover ourselves and our subjects with our students, we make ourselves, as well as our subjects, vulnerable to indifference, judgment, ridicule."[15] As previously discussed, Palmer sees the early departure of many teachers from the profession as an outcome of overwhelming circumstances like these. This is unfortunate because most people who enter into teaching are moved to do so by a passion or an inner call to do the work. The genesis of the passion can reveal itself in different ways. Sometimes one is fascinated by and becomes passionate about a subject. For some, that passion leads to a desire to want to teach. Palmer writes: "Sometimes we are drawn to a particular subject because it sheds light on our identity as well as on the world: "We did not merely find a subject to teach—the subject also found us."[16]

The narrative in *The Courage to Teach* has a sustained focus on the practice and experiences associated with teaching, and offers ways for the devoted teacher to tune in to their inner life. Palmer warns teachers that it is critical to take measures to strengthen the inner self, or one risks entering a world that will invariably challenge and erode the inner spirit. *The Courage to Teach* is also "an exploration of the inner landscape" of Palmer's life, as it relates to his experiences of losing and regaining heart in teaching.[17] Losing heart, as Palmer illuminates, "is grief that may mask itself as boredom, sullenness, or anger, but is, at bottom, a cry for meaning."[18] As with most of his work, he shares his wounds and offers them as a source of healing.

One of the wounds he shares occurred during a very difficult year in his teaching career. Although he tried in many ways, he could not connect with his students. To add to the burden, Palmer received the devastating news of his father's sudden death. Shattered by the loss, and living far from the comfort of friends and family to console him, he recalls walking into the classroom and facing the ever-present sense of defeat and isolation that each day brought. He writes, "Every day I had to climb a mountain

---

15. Palmer, *Courage to Teach*, 18.
16. Palmer, *Courage to Teach*, 26.
17. Palmer, *Seeking Vocation*, 5.
18. Palmer, *Seeking Vocation*, 8.

of personal grief . . . to drag myself back into the classroom."[19] He states, "I would not repeat that year for fame or money, but it left me with a pearl of great price: . . . a deepened empathy for teachers whose daily work is as much about climbing mountains as it is about teaching and learning."[20]

My personal transformation developed from the many perplexing situations and disappointments that I experienced as a teacher. These include classes that went poorly despite my preparation, and receiving criticism instead of support from superiors. These experiences have humbled me and have led me towards establishing a personal relationship with God, as there was literally no one else to turn to. As difficult as my career transition has been, I came to understand that this new juncture in my life was where I was placed for a purpose, a purpose that is continually revealing itself.

Through Palmer's work, I learned invaluable lessons about being a teacher. I learned about what it means to have the courage to teach when life deals its terrible blows and one still has to face a classroom full of students. The illnesses and deaths of my parents devastated me. The experience led to despair and a seemingly endless tunnel of darkness. Yet, I had to work. I learned about how one's inner feelings are projected outward into the world, for better or for worse. I learned how one's sorrow can never be fully masked and how that emotion can be misinterpreted and work against oneself in a school environment. I learned that, to be most effective, the art of teaching requires inner peace. This is a state of mind that I am able to maintain only in intimate communion with God.

I believe that it was when I humbled myself before God that I became a better teacher. I acknowledged God as the center of my life. This newfound relationship with God helped me to heal from the tragedy of having lost several loved ones, and to be fully present to my students. I became a much better listener, the catalyst to better teaching. Palmer's work has been like a beacon guiding me to this sacred and rich interior place.

In writing about his own journey towards God, Palmer seems to describe this part of my life story in his 2000 book, *Let Your Life Speak: Listening for the Voice of Vocation*. He writes that the spiritual journey is filled with paradoxes and that humility is central to this journey. He adds that the path to humility leads some people through humiliation: the kind of humiliation that allows one to grow from the ground up. Palmer notes that when one finds God it is usually not up in the heavens, but down in the

---

19. Palmer, *Courage to Teach*, xi.
20. Palmer, *Courage to Teach*, xii.

The Spirituality of Teaching

depths of one's sorrow. And when one encounters God, one is lifted up. In his experience, as in mine, he emerged from his sorrow with clarity about selfhood and vocation.[21]

In addition to isolation, Palmer found that in higher education there was little to no meaningful interaction between faculty members. However, this is true at all levels of education. It is also my observation that the culture of the academy does not support meaningful interactions related to improving one's teaching. Why? One reason is that faculty meetings focus on administrative issues, curriculum, technology, assessments, etc. Such discussions are compressed into very short meetings, and therefore conversations about the craft of teaching, or expressions of concerns about teaching, are rare. Another reason is that teaching schedules rarely allow for interaction amongst teachers. Teachers seldom see each other over the course of the day. When they do meet one another, it is generally for a brief moment before rushing off to the next class.

Isolation, Palmer notes, is one of many divisive structures in educational institutions. He posits that, "The external structures of education would not have the power to divide us as deeply as they do, if they were not rooted in one of the most compelling features of our inner landscape—fear."[22] He defines fear as "an obverse sign of our emotional need for community. Our fears arise from the sense that community is not present or possible, that we are not related to each other in a way that allows us to be vulnerable without being damaged."[23]

Palmer maintains, "Education is a fearful enterprise," affecting all participants.[24] Early on, students become riddled with fear; they are afraid of failure, and of ridicule from others. These fears often lead those "born with a love of learning, to hate the idea of school. For the teacher, fear is equally prevalent."[25] However, the fear could be assuaged if communal support existed in the academy. As he recollects,

> When a class that has gone badly comes to a merciful end, I am fearful long after it is over . . . From where I stood, exposed and vulnerable at the front of the room, my students seemed enviously safe, hidden behind their notebooks, anonymous in the midst of

21. Palmer, *Let Your Life Speak*, 56–57, 70.
22. Palmer, *Courage to Teach*, 36.
23. Palmer, *To Know as We Are Known*, 85.
24. Palmer, *Courage to Teach*, 36.
25. Palmer, *Courage to Teach*, 36.

69

the crowd ... When my students' fears mix with mine, fear multiplies ... and education is paralyzed.[26]

According to Palmer, fear and isolation contribute to the paradox of teaching that the person who successfully teaches one day is the same one who fails as a teacher the next. I believe that if teachers were to have opportunities to share these experiences without fear of being ridiculed or penalized, it would help create fellowship. Another critical element is that this open, honest sharing would help bolster one's self-esteem. Unfortunately, fear of being labeled a failure prevents most faculty members from this kind of openness. Palmer is astute in his assessment of this reality. He writes, "The divisive structures would not exist if it were not for the fact that we collaborate with them. We collaborate out of fear."[27] In speaking for himself, on the surface, his fear was about losing his "job or image or status" if he did not "pay homage to institutional powers." He notes, "Fear is nearly universal in the relations of faculty and administration, and fear is a standard management tool in too many administrative kit bags."[28]

As Palmer went deeper into the issues of fear and divisiveness, he learned that his collaboration with the divisive structures had a spiritual component: it stemmed from "fear of encounters with the truth."[29] Palmer states, "Humans fear encounters in which the other is free to be itself, to speak its own truth, to tell us what we may not wish to hear."[30] He explains, "We want those encounters on our own terms, so that we can control their outcomes, so that they will not threaten our view of world and self."[31] He asserts that the structure of academic institutions is such that one can insulate oneself from any possibility of a real relationship: "To avoid a live encounter with teachers, students can hide behind their notebooks and their silence. To avoid a live encounter with students, teachers can hide behind their podiums, their credentials, their power. To avoid a live encounter with one another, faculty can hide behind their academic specialties."[32]

Most notably, Palmer writes about the "pretense of objectivity," which manages one's fear. For him, objectivity is a way "to avoid a live encounter

26. Palmer, *Courage to Teach*, 37.
27. Palmer, *Courage to Teach*, 37.
28. Palmer, *Courage to Teach*, 36.
29. Palmer, *Courage to Teach*, 37.
30. Palmer, *Courage to Teach*, 37.
31. Palmer, *Courage to Teach*, 38.
32. Palmer, *Courage to Teach*, 38.

with subjects of study, teachers and students alike."[33] He discovered that through the objective way of knowing and teaching, students could easily say, "'Don't ask me to think about this stuff—just give me the facts,'" and faculty can say, "'Here are the facts—don't think about them, just get them straight.'"[34] This avoidance is the null curriculum in schools, a curriculum that is absent rather than explicit.[35] Later in this chapter, I explore the concept of objective ways of knowing in more detail.

What to do in the face of such fear? In *The Courage to Teach*, Palmer offers an interesting and challenging idea. He maintains that if one loses heart in teaching and wants to regain it, one must get more involved in the teaching experience.[36] The teaching experience consists of three important sources. First are the subjects one teaches. The breadth and scope of the subjects one teaches make it impossible for anyone to master them fully. Therefore, one's knowledge of them is never complete. Second are the students one teaches. According to Palmer, "they are larger than life and even more complex."[37] If we add the fact that teachers have to interact with dozens of students at a time, and sometimes with over a hundred on any given day, the complexity of the task grows exponentially. The third, most neglected source are the teachers themselves. Pointing out this lack of attention to the teacher is one of Palmer's singular contributions to field of education.

Susan Black, whose research on teaching appears in the 2001 article, "A Lifeboat for New Teachers," finds a continuing trend that demonstrates a lack of support or interest in the well-being of new teachers. Her research indicates that new teachers often feel that "they are left to sink or swim," citing a lack of support or guidance for their response. Parallel to Palmer's findings, the research showed that as a result of this, thirty percent of new teachers and up to fifty percent of new teachers in urban schools leave the profession after three years, and nine percent leave before finishing their first year of teaching.[38] Black also reports that within her sample base, the teachers who remained in the profession long-term were typically those who received help in the form of mentors. However, her research shows

33. Palmer, *Courage to Teach*, 38.
34. Palmer, *Courage to Teach*, 38.
35. Eisner, *Educational Imagination*, 97.
36. Palmer, *Courage to Teach*, 2.
37. Palmer, *Courage to Teach*, 2.
38. Black, "Lifeboat for New Teachers," 46.

that across the country, well-organized induction programs consisting of mentor and peer support are the exception rather than the rule.[39]

The third variable at play in learning about teaching is fundamental to Palmer's theory and is one I've already mentioned: "We teach who we are."[40] He writes, "Teaching, like any truly human activity, emerges from one's inwardness, for better or worse. As I teach, I project the condition of my soul onto my students, my subject, and our way of being together. The entanglements I experience in the classroom are often no more or less than the convolutions of my inner life. Viewed from this angle, teaching holds a mirror to the soul."[41]

According to Palmer, the convolutions of the inner life develop from living a divided life. Integrity refers to being in the world in a way that is integral to one's nature. This concept, which is at the center of Palmer's theory of living an undivided life, demonstrates the influence of Thomas Merton. Merton wrote: "A tree gives glory to God by being a tree. For in being what God means it to be it is obeying Him. It 'consents,' so to speak to His creative love . . . therefore a tree imitates God by being a tree."[42] To help distinguish between how God has created humans to be as opposed to the outside forces that sway one in other directions, Palmer advises readers to reflect upon what is life-giving and what drains one's life away. For in order to teach as authentic individuals, one first has to know one's true self and one's true needs.[43]

For Palmer, identity and integrity reflect all aspects, both positive and negative, of one's personality, experiences, and perceptions. He reminds his readers that "the self is not infinitely elastic," meaning that individuals have limitations as well as strengths and that integrity far outweighs technique.[44] However, he does not dismiss techniques altogether. For him, technique has value in that the techniques one chooses reveal something about one's true nature, adding authenticity to one's work.[45]

Fettered imaging is what Palmer exposes and cautions against. But can a person ever be completely "unfettered" by cultural norms? I think

---

39. Black, "Lifeboat for New Teachers," 47.
40. Palmer, *Courage to Teach*, 2.
41. Palmer, *Courage to Teach*, 3.
42. Merton, *New Seeds of Contemplation*, 29.
43. Palmer, *Courage to Teach*, 14.
44. Palmer, *Courage to Teach*, 12.
45. Palmer, *Courage to Teach*, 25.

not. One can also argue that not all cultural norms are negative. The journey into the self ought to reveal the outside influences that impede one from becoming authentic as well as those that have a positive influence on one's sense of self. In the process of self-discovery, a healthy, maturing adult should be able to discern which external influences they want to embrace and which ones to reject.

Palmer holds that it is not possible to know students or a subject well unless one truly knows one's self. He writes,

> Knowing my students and my subject depends heavily on self-knowledge. When I do not know myself, I cannot know who my students are. I will see them through a glass darkly, in the shadows of my unexamined life—and when I cannot see them clearly, I cannot teach them well. When I do not know myself, I cannot know my subject—not at the deepest levels of embodied, personal meaning . . . Good teaching requires self-knowledge: it is a secret hidden in plain sight.[46]

Given the importance of the teacher having a healthy inner life, Palmer advocates that learning to foster it should become part of the professional curriculum for new teachers. Not only that, the selfhood of the teacher should also become a standard topic of discussion and exploration in the movement toward educational reform. He argues: "In our rush to reform education, we have forgotten a simple truth: Reform will never be achieved by renewing appropriations, restructuring schools, rewriting curricula, and revising texts if we continue to demean and dishearten the human resource called the teacher on whom so much depends."[47] He asks: "How can schools educate students if they fail to support the teacher's inner life?"[48] After examining the issue from various angles, Palmer contends that part of what needs to change is rooted in contemporary epistemology.

PARKER J. PALMER ON THE NATURE OF KNOWLEDGE

In 1993, Palmer delivered a lecture at Berea College in Kentucky entitled, "The Violence of Our Knowledge: Toward a Spirituality of Higher Education." In it, he shared some of his thinking about the nature of authentic

---

46. Palmer, *Courage to Teach*, 3.
47. Palmer, *Courage to Teach*, 4.
48. Palmer, *Courage to Teach*, 6.

knowing. He distinguished three weak points of contemporary epistemology: its objective, analytic, and experimental qualities.[49] According to Palmer, these three points undergird the Western mode of knowing. He emphasized that he is not opposed to these modes of knowing, simply that he prefers a balanced approach. For Palmer, "true higher learning involves a healthy dance between the objective and the subjective, between the analytic and the integrative, between the experimental and the subjective."[50]

According to Palmer, the spirituality of learning, or a "transformed understanding of knowing," comes from four components. He contends that: "learning is personal, learning is communal, learning is reciprocal, and learning is transformational."[51] He shares a story that helps to explain his theory, which dates back to a chapter in Native American history during the 1700s. The white commissioners of the Virginia territory presented a treaty to the Indians of Six Nations. As part of the treaty, these Native Americans "were invited to send their young men to the College of William and Mary, one of the first institutions of higher learning established in the Colony."[52]

The elders of the tribe took the treaty home and contemplated its offer. The following day, the tribal leaders returned with their decision. The following is their response to the white commissioners, as rendered in the account upon which Palmer draws:

> We know that you highly esteem the kind of learning taught in your colleges, and that the maintenance of our young men while with you would be very expensive to you. We are convinced that you mean to do us good by your proposal, and we thank you heartily. But you, who are wise, must know that different nations have different conceptions of things, and you will therefore not take it amiss if our ideas of education happen not to be the same as yours. We have had some experience of it. Several of our young people were brought up at the colleges of the Northern Provinces. They were instructed in all your sciences, but when they came back to us, they were bad runners, ignorant of every means of living in the woods, neither fit for hunters nor counselors, they were totally good for nothing. We are, however, not the less obliged by your kind offer, though we decline accepting it. But to show our grateful

49. Palmer, "Violence of Our Knowledge," 3.
50. Palmer, "Violence of Our Knowledge," 1.
51. Palmer, "Violence of Our Knowledge," 1.
52. Palmer, "Violence of Our Knowledge," 2.

sense of it, if the gentlemen of Virginia will send us a dozen of their sons, we will take care of their education, instruct them in all we know, and make men of them.[53]

Palmer read this dialogue and deciphered a deeper, richer meaning embedded within the exchange. In his hermeneutic, the story revealed a profoundly spiritual way of perceiving human life. He notes, "This story has a voice of humor, a voice of quiet wisdom, and a voice of deep insight."[54] The white commissioners assumed they were negotiating with "unlettered" tribal elders. In reality, they were dealing with men who possessed a level of wisdom that white Americans do not yet have. "What these tribal elders knew," he observes, "was that every way of knowing becomes a way of living."[55] They understood, in their own language, that "every epistemology becomes an ethic."[56] According to Palmer, they also knew deep down inside, that the battle over territory and resources was not the only thing for which they were fighting. Deeper and more fundamental was the war over "whose way of knowing would prevail, as formative and shaping of the lives of human beings."[57]

The "objectivist" way of knowing—the first of the three dimensions that Palmer discusses—was the mode that prevailed. In *To Know as We Are Known: Education as a Spiritual Journey*, Palmer claims that to determine the foundation of any culture in question, one need only ask: Where do reality and power reside?[58] He asserts that in Western culture, it resides in outside events, objects, and science. For Westerners, manipulating objects and events gives a sense of power. He maintains that there is a connection between the way one approaches knowing and one's capacity for violence, the kind of violence that "always involves violating the integrity of the other."[59] Using Merton's expression, he argues that the mode of knowing practiced in the academy has resulted in "a subtle, but pervasive form of violence to our personal and social lives."[60]

---

53. Spiller et al., *Wayfinding Leadership*, 31–32.
54. Palmer, "Violence of Our Knowledge," 2.
55. Palmer, "Violence of Our Knowledge," 2.
56. Palmer, "Violence of Our Knowledge," 2.
57. Palmer, "Violence of Our Knowledge," 3.
58. Palmer, *To Know as We Are Known*, 20.
59. Palmer, *To Know as We Are Known*, 3.
60. Palmer, *To Know as We Are Known*, 3.

According to Palmer, "objective means that you cannot know anything truly and well, unless you know it at arm's length, at a distance, at great remove."[61] Within our dominant epistemology, he believes, is a deep-seated fear of what is perceived as "subjectivism," which implies revealing one's true self and allowing the other to do so as well (as the letter writers above understood so well). "Subjectivism" can become quite dangerous. We see this today with what is often referred to as "alternative facts." This refers to individuals deciding about which randomly quoted "facts" they will believe based on their own subjective preferences, and not on objective reality. Palmer views objectivism as a necessary response to such untamed subjectivism. However, he argues, "we are at a time in history when we have to understand that unfettered objectivism is equally as cruel as unfettered subjectivism."[62]

The work of John Dewey influenced Palmer's thinking about objectivity. In 1897, Dewey wrote his pedagogical creed, in which he stated, "I believe that one of the greatest difficulties in the present teaching of science is that the material is presented in purely objective form . . . It should be introduced, not so much as new subject matter, but as showing the factors already involved in previous experience . . ."[63] He maintained that the changes that occurred during the industrial revolution not only changed how one lives, but also how one thinks and constructs reality.

The industrial revolution ushered in an era in which the speed of productivity became of utmost importance. While the public in general benefited from having material things mass produced, readily available, and cheaper, Dewey saw how this fast-paced activity led to less and less engagement between humans and the world and things around them. Dewey argues that everything in life is a process, not a simple thoughtless action. As Palmer would agree, Dewey favors the structure of the pre-industrial age because community was valued. Labor required a communal process and hands-on involvement. For Dewey, this involved experience with the nature of things, which he felt developed character, discipline, and responsibility.[64] On the other hand, both Dewey and Palmer recognize the value of the advancements in science. Scientific achievements have helped increase one's knowledge of things and have enabled humans to accomplish things

---

61. Palmer, *To Know as We Are Known*, 3.
62. Palmer, *To Know as We Are Known*, 4.
63. Dewey, "My Pedagogic Creed," 26–27.
64. Dworkin, "School and Society," 36, 37.

that were once only a fantasy. The Internet, cell phones, the development of vaccinations against and cures for deadly diseases are but some examples.

"Analytic" is the second dimension of Western knowing that Palmer examines. Analytic means taking the object to be studied and breaking it apart to determine how the object works. According to Palmer, this way of knowing "has created a great facility to take things apart, but very little capacity for the creative or integrative act of putting things back together."[65] For example, it was not until he became a community organizer that he understood what a family was like. As a trained sociologist, his prior analytic understanding of the average family was that it consisted of 2.8 people—a dissected, objective view of family. These kinds of experiences led him to view analytic as a kind of "knowledge that lends itself to the violence of dissecting everything so that the center cannot hold."[66]

The third way of knowing is "experimental." Once an object has been objectified and dissected, the knower is now free to maneuver the pieces in an attempt to create something new, a creation that is more in line with what the knower thinks the world ought to be. Palmer stresses that he is not against great science. Indeed, he honors it. What he opposes is the experimental, Western approach to allegedly under-resourced cultures, where one looks to impose "one's politics, dimensions of economy, or religious understanding, in order to make those countries more pleasing to our eyes."[67] He considers this a type of experimentation that goes "beyond the legitimacy of the laboratory."[68]

Objective, analytic, and experimental ways of knowing are not merely philosophical abstractions. These ways of knowing are evident in one's daily life. One example Palmer cites is the Carnegie Commission survey of recent college graduates in the United States. When asked about the shape of the global society, 90 percent of the students responded with negativity and pessimism for our planet. Yet, the same 90 percent said they personally see a bright future for themselves.[69] Rejecting the objectivist way of knowing, Palmer writes, "They have been so thoroughly schooled in an objectivist view of the world that they don't even know that their dismal facts and figures are about the very planet that they walk upon day in and day out.

65. Palmer, "Violence of Our Knowledge," 6.
66. Palmer, "Violence of Our Knowledge," 6.
67. Palmer, "Violence of Our Knowledge," 6.
68. Palmer, "Violence of Our Knowledge," 6.
69. Levine, *When Dreams and Heroes Died*, 103–5.

How could they, when the information has been presented to them at such great remove?"[70]

Another example is how Palmer was initially taught, at great remove, about the Third Reich and the slaughter of millions of Jewish people. He writes, "it had happened, I knew that for a fact, but it was presented to me at such objective distance, so disconnected from the facts of my own life, that at a feeling level I ended up with a sense of 'another planet and another species.'"[71] The curriculum omitted information about the lives of the victims; it ignored stories of great poets, artists, and intellectuals among them. In his experience, the school dealt with the Holocaust as an abstraction.

Palmer also believes that the Western concept of truth lies in experimentation, a kind of truth-seeking that can "lead to self-destruction."[72] He points to the documentary "The Day After Trinity," which describes what scientists knew before detonating the first atomic weapon. He recalls a chilling moment in the production, during an interview with a mathematician who stated that, "'the day before we pushed the button on that nuclear weapon, we had done calculations to indicate there was a small but very real possibility that when we set it off there would be an instant incineration of the entire envelope of oxygen surrounding the earth, thus snuffing out life on earth. Still we went ahead and pushed the button.'"[73]

In examples from the development of nuclear weapons and other realms, Palmer asserts that the appeal of objectivism is that it gives the knower a sense of superiority. "The real agenda driving objectivism is arrogance and control."[74] In the Western mode of thinking, disconnection is valued to the point where it is viewed as "an intellectual virtue."[75] Here he agrees with educational curriculum theorist Eliot Eisner, who writes: "The overall aim, rooted in the Enlightenment, was to create an objectively detached true description of the world as it really is. American educators, and particularly American educational psychologists, saw promise in these methods, for with them educational practice itself could become a scientifically guided activity."[76] It is this philosophy of education that Parker

---

70. Palmer, "Violence of Our Knowledge," 7.
71. Palmer, "Violence of Our Knowledge," 7.
72. Palmer, "Violence of Our Knowledge," 8.
73. Palmer, *To Know as We Are Known*, 1.
74. Palmer, *Courage to Teach*, 57.
75. Palmer, *Courage to Teach*, 65.
76. Eisner, *Educational Imagination*, 196.

The Spirituality of Teaching

Palmer resisted, arguing instead that we be attentive to ways of thinking and knowing that support both the need and capacity for connectedness—"on which good teaching depends."[77]

Given that Palmer saw an imbalance in the way education is approached, the aim of his theories has been to re-balance the scale.[78] He saw signs of hope in our current times. In various disciplines, there are new thinkers who stand in opposition to the way of knowing called objectivism. A new intellectual movement has been growing organically. He notes that within the new intellectual movement are feminist philosophers who are taking a new approach to how science is done, and to how the story is told—from the inside. This means immersing oneself in the reality of that which is being studied, in order to understand it. Palmer would call this doing science with "appreciative receptivity."[79]

For Palmer, "Great thinking in all fields at its deepest and best is connective activity, a community-building activity, and not an activity which is meant to distance and alienate us."[80] There is also ecological science, which re-introduces students to the notion that humans are to be stewards of the earth, "that they are not apart from nature, they are a part of nature, and in conversation with nature."[81] He observes that "this revolution is also happening in subatomic physics where the separation between the knower and the known has been discarded."[82] He revels in this finding: "To hear physicists say things like, 'It is no longer possible to make a statement about nature that is not also a statement about myself,' is to hear the myth of objectivism crack and crumble."[83]

Palmer agrees with the importance of sensation and rationality, the way of knowing strongly supported by the Enlightenment cultures, and the contributions of modern science. However, he insists that the educational practice of teaching and learning with all of one's senses be given a place of preeminence. He advocates teaching to and from the totality of the person, arguing that teaching should appeal to one's many faculties: intuition,

---

77. Palmer, *Courage to Teach*, 65.
78. Palmer, *Courage to Teach*, 64.
79. Palmer, "Violence of Our Knowledge," 9.
80. Palmer, "Violence of Our Knowledge," 9.
81. Palmer, "Violence of Our Knowledge," 10.
82. Palmer, "Violence of Our Knowledge," 10.
83. Palmer, "Violence of Our Knowledge," 10.

empathy, emotion, and faith, along with sensation and rationality. This, he asserts, expands one's capacity to teach and learn.

Eisner shares this perspective about appealing to the many human faculties, and gives this example:

> What can be known, say, about autumn can take form in scientific propositions that deal with chemical changes in trees, in astronomical propositions about the location of our planet in relation to the sun, in poetic expression disclosing the smell of burning autumn leaves, in visual images that present to our consciousness the color of a Vermont landscape, and in auditory forms that capture the crackle of leaves under our footsteps.[84]

In summary, Palmer and others advocate for the recognition of multiple modes of knowing and holistic knowing. Why? Because recognizing the various modes of learning by which individuals process information can help transform how one approaches teaching as well as student assessments. The implications for education are wide and deep.

THE MOVEMENT IN ACTION: REIMAGINING EDUCATION

A critical step toward creating innovative ways of learning is to reimagine the way one teaches and learns. For Palmer and others, imaging is what creates our reality. As an undergraduate majoring in philosophy and sociology, he was introduced to C. Wright Mills's idea of the "social imagination" and was so captivated by it that decades later he is still making reference to it. From Mills's work Palmer learned that one's view of the world depends on the lenses through which one sees. For example, viewed from the angle of social theory, he was surprised to see the conditioned responses and non-verbal cues that form one's social life, and have such power over one.[85] Palmer then began to highlight the critical importance of knowing the power that social influences can have on one if one leads an unexamined life.

The notion of an unexamined life piqued Palmer's interest in Mills's concept of on-stage and backstage realities. The distinction is that the on-stage show is promoted by the forces of social control, and the backstage reality (discussed in the previous chapter) mirrors the great divide in one's

---

84. Eisner, *Educational Imagination*, 147.
85. Palmer, *Courage to Teach*, 27.

inner life. The theory also helped Palmer to think differently about education and adopt new lenses through which to view it. He was able to see the academy through the lens of a sociologist. He viewed the academy as an institution with great influence on each of its members, not all of which was positive. For example, he saw an unsettling degree of control over how faculty members were to respond to one another and to their students, and his years within the academy taught him that this control brought about a conditioned response that was extremely difficult to break through.

When viewed through a different lens, he found that it is possible for a transformed pedagogy to reach the institutional level. That is, when individuals refuse to support the structures that diminish them as people and instead begin to form alliances with like-minded others, large-scale change can happen. Drawing from observations of the civil rights movement and the feminist movement, Palmer notes, "Historically, significant social change has *only* been achieved in the face of massive institutional opposition."[86] The process of institutional change is generally long and difficult. When organizations resist and retaliate against non-conformers, some reformers are likely to abandon their cause. However, there are others who are energized by institutional resistance. Palmer refers to this as a "movement mentality."[87]

The movement mentality develops because the systems' resistance becomes an added catalyst for change, not a deterrent. In other words, in this mentality, change happens despite institutional resistance, because it is the resistance itself that helps fuel the change. The adversarial condition itself tells one that there is something inherently wrong that needs to be corrected. It encourages both sides to seek solutions and envision new horizons. One example is the change that occurred as a result of the Civil Rights Movement. There was a time in our history where the segregation of African Americans and white Americans led to separating one from the other in places such as drinking water fountains and restaurants. The organized protests and actions of African-American citizens fueled the change towards ridding the country of this abuse of human rights, fostering national legislation to implement civil rights (see chapter 2 for more on Palmer's discussion of this example).

The feminist movement is a prime example of how resistance can actually create momentum towards a cause. Unfortunately, it seems that most

---

86. Palmer, *Courage to Teach*, 170.
87. Palmer, *Courage to Teach*, 171.

of women's efforts for social transformation toward gender equality in the U.S. are marked by resistance from the male-dominated institutions. It was only a few decades before the Women's Liberation Movement began that women had no right to vote in the United States. However, as resistance grew, women not only earned this right, but were able to venture into areas formerly prized as exclusively male domains—notably the workforce.[88]

In addition, the "movement mentality" of which Palmer speaks is often sparked by the power of one person speaking out. Such is the case of the current "Me Too" movement, which developed into a force that its male opponents could not squelch. American activist Tarana Burke of Bronx, New York, founded the movement in 2006 particularly to help women of color voice and counter sexual assault. The movement was in essence about survivors helping survivors, or healing oneself and others by sharing one's wounds. In 2017 a few catalytic actions set the movement on a more expansive course, to include women of all races and cultures. The "Me Too" movement went viral through social media as several women took a public stand against powerful men who victimized them sexually. The aggressors were generally men in positions of power. As a result of the "Me Too" movement, the landscape of the work environment is beginning to show positive changes for women.

At this moment in our history, teaching and learning for transformation is crucial for survival. Ours is an era in which some people have taken truth hostage, where facts are randomly and arbitrarily distorted, and where violence is encouraged and democracy threatened. Furthermore, this is happening amidst the COVID pandemic, which has claimed millions of lives worldwide, particularly in communities of color.

In addition, African American communities are living with a heightened sense of danger amidst social unrest triggered by racial injustices. We are experiencing moments that are similar to the 1960s, when the Reverend Dr. Martin Luther King Jr. led the Civil Rights Movement. The current social unrest was triggered by the recent brutal killings of African Americans, which over the last centuries has oftentimes been an unpunishable (or at least unpunished) crime in this country.

Particular events in the summer of 2020 ignited the current tensions, notably the killings of three African American individuals: George Floyd, Breonna Taylor, and Ahmaud Arbery. This led to numerous protests throughout the United States and quickly became a global phenomenon

---

88. Harper, *History of Woman Suffrage*, 12–25.

known as the Black Lives Matter Movement. This movement began formally in 2013 with Alicia Garza, Patrisse Cullors, and Opal Tometi. Together, the three women founded Black Lives Matter as a Black-centered political movement, in response to the acquittal of Trayvon Martin's murderer, George Zimmerman. Seven years later, seemingly nothing has changed with regards to police killings of African-American citizens. In the summer of 2020 we saw protests against such killings that were largely peaceful. In some instances, looting and violence took place, but in most other instances it was the police who turned against the protesters in violent force.

Many university and school leaders began to reflect on these incidents and to express a renewed commitment to racial justice. Among them were Jesuit institutions, including my own. As such, conversations of social injustice are coming to the forefront and many forms of racism have been exposed in the public arena. It is becoming more apparent to many that racism exists in two ways: the blatantly obvious kind, and the more covert, systemic kind.

Teaching religious studies affords me the opportunity to make these issues central in class discussions and reading assignments. Students look to their teachers for answers and find comfort in knowing that their concerns are being addressed. Students also want a forum for discussion and the subject of religion lends itself to healthy and respectful exchanges of ideas. Despite the inevitable occasions where racism is obvious in the school, I find it heartwarming to see how much love does, in fact, exist among the students of all races and ethnic backgrounds. Students at the high school age are in that phase of life where they are idealistic and emotional about injustices.

To say that racism is systemic in the institution does not negate the fact that there are many students (and faculty) who do not fall in that category and who stand in solidarity to challenge the status quo. These are individuals who stand on their personal convictions of what is right, exercise their beliefs, and would not condone but, on the contrary, would voice objection to the negative behavior of others. Students of color witness this and appreciate it. Showing the students that powerful voices surround them in their struggle is something that they not only appreciate, but that also makes them feel safe.

According to Palmer, "the genius of social movements is paradoxical."[89] In many instances, reformers have to withdraw from the oppressive

---

89. Palmer, *Courage to Teach*, 172.

institution in order to gain strength. It is with that strength that they can return and institute changes. He notes, "Both the civil rights and women's movements had to free themselves from racist and sexist organizations in order to generate power. Then, with that power, they returned to change the lay, and the law of the land."[90]

For Palmer, such movements have four definable stages of development. In the first stage, individuals have made the decision to live authentically and to cultivate a life of inner strength and harmony through a private, personal journey, which generally takes place outside of institutions. In the second stage, groups of like-minded individuals begin to form and develop shared visions and strategy. In the third stage, these communities go public, bringing awareness to the issues at hand, leaving themselves open to constructive criticism that will help refine their mission. In the fourth stage, individuals experience "alternative rewards," which they receive through peer support and the development of new institutional projects that may result from the movement.[91]

Since publishing *The Courage to Teach*, Palmer has witnessed "solid evidence that a movement to reclaim the relevance of the teacher's and learner's inner lives, has become more visible, credible, and compelling."[92] However, he does not credit his work as the catalyst for this movement. He acknowledges that the movement toward change has had a long history. Its seeds were planted by like-minded people who gathered in community to reinforce their beliefs and who went public with their ideas. He posits that once a movement becomes public, it can grow, although perhaps not as quickly as one might like.

The movement for educational reform has a long way to go towards achieving major goals. However, Palmer notes that today, major national organizations are aligning themselves with topics of spirituality in education, and organizing around the values of deep reform. In earlier work, he names institutions that began this work, and which have continued to innovate educational reform. They include: The American Association of Higher Education, the Association for General and Liberal Studies, and the Professional and Organizational Development Network in Higher

---

90. Palmer, *Courage to Teach*, 172.
91. Palmer, *Courage to Teach*, 173.
92. Palmer, *Courage to Teach*, 191.

Education.[93] Palmer believes that institutions like these, with their renewed vision, point to a sign of hope in the great venture of education.

PARKER J. PALMER'S THEORY OF EDUCATION

Palmer's style of teaching is imbued with a sense of spirituality. He adopts a humanistic approach to education in which an ongoing dialogue between teachers and students is essential. This approach is equally reflected in Gabriel Moran's work: "Insofar as teaching refers to interaction in the human community, teaching is always a form of conversation. To be taught as a human being is simply to enter the human conversation."[94]

Conversation is at the center of how Palmer designs a classroom session. In constructing the design, he focuses on "six paradoxical tensions" that for him are key in forming the appropriate classroom environment.[95] He does not view these as the panacea for large-scale educational reform, but offers them as an illustration of how the principle of paradox might inform individual teachers' pedagogical practice. He writes that this "is not a formula, but a personal account" of what works for him.[96] His readers may find that some of these modes of teaching work for them as well. It is important to note that in his theory of education, Palmer does not speak about changing school curriculum. Rather, he addresses the ways in which to navigate paradox in the classroom environment, so that both teacher and students are immersed in the process of teaching and learning.

First, he writes, the teaching and learning space "should be bounded and open." Boundaries create order and structure. Without them, the classroom becomes "a chaotic void, and in such a place, no learning is likely to occur."[97] He creates boundaries by using various tools to sustain the focus on the subject at hand: questions, a text, or data. Within those guidelines, he notes, "students are free to speak," but the guidelines (not just the teacher) serve to direct the conversation toward the subject.

Second, Palmer believes that "the space should be hospitable and 'charged.'"[98] He finds that students respond best and are more open in a

---

93. Palmer, *Courage to Teach*, 181.
94. Moran, *Showing How*, 124.
95. Palmer, *Courage to Teach*, 76.
96. Palmer, *Courage to Teach*, 80.
97. Palmer, *Courage to Teach*, 77.
98. Palmer, *Courage to Teach*, 77.

space they perceive to be welcoming and safe. He adds, "Hospitality in the classroom requires not only that we treat our students with civility and compassion, but also, that we invite our students and their insights into the conversation."[99] Safety, in this context, implies that students are free to express themselves and feel safe if they are wrong or if others disagree with them. What is important is that students are "feeling the challenge and risks inherent in pursuing the deep things of the world, or of the soul."[100]

Third, "the space should invite the voice of the individual, and the voice of the group."[101] He focuses on creating a space where the authentic voice of the student is heard, regardless of whether others agree with what is said. In this space, the voice of the group is in dialogue with the voice of the individual. For Palmer, real learning then occurs when "the group can affirm, question, challenge, and correct the voice of the individual."[102] His role as teacher is to moderate the activity by listening and repeating what is said.

In this exchange, the group can hear itself more clearly, and may, at times, decide "even [to] change its own collective mind."[103] This paradox reinforces Palmer's understanding that teaching, learning, and knowing happen through intimacy. For him, knowing is relational, and "at its deepest reaches, knowing is always communal."[104]

According to Palmer, the paradox of individual and collective voices has power on two levels: (1) "A corporate voice emerges through honest dialogue," and (2) each individual learns to be more reflective before and after they enter the conversation.[105] He notes, "In a learning space shaped by this paradox, not only do students learn about a subject, but they also learn to speak their own thoughts about that subject, and to listen for an emergent, collective wisdom that may influence their ideas and beliefs."[106]

Running parallel to this is the fourth paradox: "The space should honor the 'little' stories of the individual and the 'big' stories of the disciplines and traditions."[107] This creates a space where students can voice some of

99. Palmer, *Courage to Teach*, 77.
100. Palmer, *Courage to Teach*, 78.
101. Palmer, *Courage to Teach*, 78.
102. Palmer, *Courage to Teach*, 78.
103. Palmer, *Courage to Teach*, 78.
104. Palmer, *Courage to Teach*, 55.
105. Palmer, *Courage to Teach*, 78.
106. Palmer, *Courage to Teach*, 79.
107. Palmer, *Courage to Teach*, 79.

The Spirituality of Teaching

their lived experiences. The space should also allow room for the student to hear their inner teacher. "The Wisdom of Students, Education for Peace and Justice, and Religious Education" by religious education scholar Harold Daly Horell gives a practical example:

> As students bring their reflections on their life experiences into dialogue with course materials, our class sessions are often transformed. They go beyond being classes *about* peace and justice education, and often become learning experiences that educate *for* greater social involvement, *for* making meaningful and morally responsible connections between our faith and our lives.[108]

Similarly, Palmer notes for his fourth paradox that personal realities are brought into conversation with the larger story of the disciplines to help one reach a better understanding of both stories. This concept flows into the fifth paradox, namely that "The space should support solitude, and surround it with the resources of community."[109] For Palmer, appropriating new material requires time alone for the student to reflect upon and absorb the information. And in a deeper sense, allowing students to be in solitude is a way to honor the integrity of their souls. However, he notes that learning is relational and, therefore, also demands community. He is a strong proponent of dialogical exchange, in which we are challenged to defend or change our thinking and in which our knowledge is thereby expanded. He comments: "This kind of exchange does not leave us alone to think our own thoughts."[110]

This approach emphasizes oral communication as the primary learning style, which is conducive for many. However, there are other people who find it difficult or impossible to engage in public discourse. On this point one might argue that in Palmer's dialogical approach, those who do not participate may well be learning through listening, hearing, and observation, or that they might more effectively demonstrate their learning through other modes besides public verbal discourse. Dewey views education in a similar manner. He sees education as the end result of living in community. One learns when one is with others and one learns through different modalities. Dewey is also perceptive about the fundamental problems inherent in the contemporary system of schooling. He writes:

---

108. Horell, "Wisdom of Students," 3–4.
109. Palmer, *Courage to Teach*, 79.
110. Palmer, *Courage to Teach*, 79.

> I believe that much of present education fails because it neglects this fundamental principle of the school as a form of community life. It conceives the school as a place where certain information is to be given, where certain lessons are to be learned, or where certain habits are to be formed. The value of these is conceived as lying largely in the remote future . . . they are mere preparation. As a result, they do not become a part of the life experience of the child and so are not truly educative.[111]

The sixth paradox is to create "a space that welcomes both silence and speech." For Palmer, speaking is not the only form of communication in teaching and learning: "We educate with silence as well."[112] Silence gives us the space to observe, process, and absorb new information. Silence is also the space in which the inner teacher appears. An important aspect in Palmer's theory is that students have the right to refuse to engage in the conversation, and they must be granted this right. I find it interesting how this paradox works because I have observed it to be true in my own teaching experience: "This permission not to speak seems to evoke speech from people who are normally silent: we are more likely to choose participation when we are granted the freedom to do so."[113] However, he notes, when silence occurs in the classroom, his theory of its value is tested. Having grown so accustomed to filling the void with speech, he too has to be aware that in breaking the silence he may be disrupting a moment of reflective learning.

The benefits Palmer gained from experiencing and reflecting on the dynamics of the six paradoxes in his own classroom teaching led him to develop and put forth his ideas. As the debates over reforming education continue, his focus is primarily on the practical aspects of teaching. Drawing from experience and his core beliefs, he designed a pedagogical practice centered on paradox. The paradoxical method is a way to develop a relational environment in the classroom, one geared toward "learning at the deepest levels."[114] This is one of Palmer's greatest contributions to the field of education: a clearly articulated, practical approach to teaching that is profoundly humanistic and deeply spiritual.

However, despite Palmer's important contribution in articulating the critical elements of how to engage students at their deepest level, there is

---

111. Dworkin, *Dewey on Education*, 22, 24.
112. Palmer, *Courage to Teach*, 80.
113. Palmer, *Courage to Teach*, 84.
114. Palmer, *Courage to Teach*, 78.

a growing population of students who will never have this experience in a classroom. This is because the most important issue of our times remains unaddressed: systemic racism in the school environment. Though Palmer has been a champion for equal rights and for putting an end to racism, this corrosive reality plagues the school system as a whole, from elementary school through the higher levels of the academy. If one is to give an example of isolation in the academy with regards to not only the teachers but students as well, fear would be at the center of the problem—the kind of fear that stokes the flames of racism.

Racism keeps certain people at arm's length from existing interactions within the academy. White privilege is what sustains systemic racism, a system that is further dominated by white, male privilege. As a Hispanic female I am keenly aware of how people of color are marginalized in all kinds of work settings, not just schools. An example that pertains to school settings is how opportunities seem to be kept within the ranks of those favored by administrators as opposed to making them known and available to the wider public.

To add to the problem, when a minority person is given an opportunity, he or she is seen as merely a token. In other words, unqualified for the opportunity. The "check-the-box" maneuver is also actively at work, meaning that when opportunities are, in fact, made known to the wider public, the end results too often show that the gesture was only a political move to appease those who might otherwise complain. Thus, the metaphoric box could be "checked" to show that the institution did the proper thing.

These racist attitudes are examples of a working philosophy that holds that if people do not perceive certain individuals as their equals, it is not possible for them to see those individuals as having anything meaningful to contribute.[115] Correspondingly, people who share these negative attitudes towards those whom they view as the "other" will never seek to engage them in an inclusive fashion.

Another example of systemic racism is the double standard that exists among students who have influential parents advocating for them versus the poor students, who tend to be students of color and have no one to speak for them. Poor students often have parents who are unavailable because they are working more than one job or do not speak the English language. One of the concerns that students of color have brought to my attention is that oftentimes students who have advocates (meaning mostly

---

115. Ellison, interview by author, video conference, May 11, 2019.

the white students) get out of difficult situations, whereas those students who do not have such advocates suffer negative consequences.

Students of color have also voiced concern over how some teachers devalue them, making them feel as if they are not part of the class. These students claim to be ignored in the classroom when they want to speak or receive abrupt responses that suggest that their thoughts or opinions are not welcome. These problems point to how insidious systemic racism is in our culture and how it seems as though no institution is free of it.

As a religious studies teacher, I am aware of how wounded some of my students are when they arrive in my classroom. Creating a safe, hospitable space for all students, regardless of their background, is of great importance to me. I do this mostly through nonverbal cues. Being approachable, friendly, open, and flexible in terms of the students' needs are a few examples of such cues. I also enjoy engaging the students where they are by talking to them about the things they like and in which they participate during their leisure time, whether sports, video games, technology, or movies. A student once paid me a great compliment by saying that he thought I was "real" and not like some other teachers, a comment I assume had to do with my habit of engaging in such normal conversations about their passions, and never holding them at arm's length. I also raise issues that are central in their lives to promote discussion—issues such as abortion, bullying, drugs, the dilemma of social media, and so on.

The problem of systemic racism creates the need for considering the third theme in Palmer's work, which is ways of teaching and learning for transformation. The message and Way of Christ anchors the subject that I teach: To love one another. It helps put into context what is happening in the world and our role in effecting the change that we want to see. I try to embody this as a teacher to the best of my ability. Research has revealed that Palmer's paradoxical theories have also, in fact, helped other teachers.

Palmer's paradoxical theory was tested in a dissertation written by James Rourke in 2010, entitled, "The Power of Paradox: How High School Teachers Perceive the Navigation of Paradox Influencing Teacher Resiliency and Student Motivation." The purpose of this study was to investigate the claims made by Palmer, in *The Courage to Teach,* that the power of paradox has a positive impact on the learning environment. Two specific and related issues—teacher resilience and student motivation—were the focal point of the investigation. The study surveyed ten teachers, and the results aligned with Palmer's theory. Rourke found that the thoughts shared by the teachers in the study supported the "contention that teachers, regardless of discipline, encounter paradox in their routines, and that the successful navigation of paradox does, in fact, enhance student motivation, and teacher resiliency."[116]

Today, Palmer has moved beyond the confines of teaching in a classroom. He views himself as a teacher in a classroom without walls, sharing his insights and experiences through books, articles, lectures, video-taped conversations, and Internet podcasts. He asks: "How can education help professionals keep their hearts alive in settings where people too often lose heart? What might help them stand up to and sometimes against the institutions from which their paychecks, and perhaps their identities, come?"[117] Merton's spiritual influence is evident in Palmer's answer. For Merton, the key question is about knowing the will of God. Merton believed, "Unnatural, frantic, anxious work, work done under pressure of greed or fear or any other inordinate passion, cannot properly speaking be dedicated to God, because God never wills such work directly."[118]

Palmer offers five "immodest proposals regarding the education of a new professional."[119] First, we must make the student teachers aware of the invisible structures that exist, and dispel the myth that these institutions have "power over our lives."[120] The invisible structures to which he refers constitute the hidden curriculum in schools. He asserts, "Institutions *are* us!" meaning that because we are the institutions, we have agency over them. Second, one must correct the disjunction between one's student teacher's emotional and intellectual intelligence by affirming the validity of both.[121] Knowledge is embedded in one's feelings. He reminds us: "In fact, science itself begins in the hunches, intuitions, and bodily knowledge that lie behind testable hypotheses."[122]

Taking this point further is his third proposal: one must teach one's students how to listen to their inner teacher for the wisdom inherent in one's feelings and emotions. He firmly believes that emotions can become sources of energy to challenge and change institutions: "Common sense

116. Rourke, "Power of Paradox," 47.
117. Palmer, *Courage to Teach*, 205.
118. Merton, *New Seeds of Contemplation*, 19.
119. Palmer, *Courage to Teach*, 208.
120. Palmer, *Courage to Teach*, 205.
121. Palmer, *Courage to Teach*, 206.
122. Palmer, *Courage to Teach*, 208.

tells us that the history of positive social change has been made *only* by people who wear their hearts on their sleeves—witness Rosa Parks, Václav Havel, Dorothy Day, and Nelson Mandela."[123]

Fourth, Palmer recommends teaching the new professionals the importance of community life in learning and achieving goals, and he offers ways to form such communities. Fifth and finally, he proposes teaching and modeling for the new professionals what it means to be "on the journey toward an undivided life, and live and work with the question of an undivided life always before them. Our students need to see how we, their elders, deal with the vagaries of fate, while refusing to sell out either our profession or our own identity and integrity."[124]

CONCLUDING THOUGHTS

Woven throughout Parker Palmer's work are the themes of identity, integrity, and personal fulfillment. Key to the development of his theory is his criticism of the Western educational system for disregarding the human aspect of learning and teaching as well as the inner life of the teacher. The focus in the Western system of education, he maintains, is on rational, objective ways of teaching, thinking, and knowing. Such an approach, he argues, creates a disconnect between the student, the teacher, the subject, and oneself, and leads both to a classroom of students who have lost interest, and a teacher who has lost heart. He advocates for modes of teaching and learning that incorporate a healthy balance of sensation and rationality. In having lived these experiences, and sharing them openly, honestly, and with humility, Palmer serves contemporary educators as a wounded healer.

His theory of education developed from lived experiences of losing and regaining heart in teaching. He articulates his theory as a pedagogy of paradox. He concludes that skillful navigation of the major paradoxes experienced in the classroom can enhance student motivation and help teachers regain the capacity to enjoy their work. He and others have found that working with these opposite poles of the paradoxes can bring a creative, vibrant energy to the classroom that can be experienced by the student and teacher alike.

Undergirding Palmer's thought process in developing his pedagogical theory is his persistent dedication to questions of purpose and meaning. He

---

123. Palmer, *Courage to Teach*, 207.
124. Palmer, *Courage to Teach*, 205, 211.

draws from ancient, spiritual wisdom as the source for understanding the human condition, and for speaking to the needs of the inner soul. Furthermore, the growing number of national organizations in education which are pursuing programs and studies to enhance spirituality in the classroom environment illuminate the growing tradition in which Palmer stands. The following chapter examines how the hermeneutic of Parker Palmer's philosophy of education can be applied to the field of religious education.

Chapter 4

CURRICULUM AND THE QUESTION OF A NEW GENERATION

IN *A HIDDEN WHOLENESS*, Parker Palmer draws upon the image of a blizzard from a Leonard Cohen song called "The Future." He evokes the terror of being cut off from one's home in the midst of a blinding storm, and then uses the image to assess the state of our world. He writes:

> There was a time when farmers on the Great Plains, at the first sign of a blizzard, would run a rope from the back door out to the barn. They all knew stories of people who had wandered off and been frozen to death, having lost sight of home in a whiteout while still in their own backyards. Today we live in a blizzard of another sort. It swirls around us as economic injustice, ecological ruin, physical and spiritual violence, and their inevitable outcome, war.[1]

The metaphor of becoming lost in our own backyards brings together four themes that Palmer has pondered for most of his adult life. The themes center on querying how this phenomenon happens and how we can find our way in the "blizzard"—or, to use Palmer's typical expression, how to move toward wholeness. The first theme addresses the importance of living authentically. The second delves into the meaning of community and the innate yearning for human connections. The third theme explores ways of teaching and learning for transformation. All of these concepts lead to the fourth theme—nonviolent social change.

In unraveling these topics, Palmer delves deeply into human spirituality. As in the blizzard metaphor, his aim is to find ways that, like the rope in the backyard, will keep one on one's intended path and return one to

---

1. Palmer, *Hidden Wholeness*, 1.

safety. Eventually, his understanding of these principles became the foundation of his pedagogical theory, which is distinctly relevant to the field of religious education.

In my opinion, in addition to his writings, the most important contribution Palmer makes to religious education is himself. There is no scarcity of religion in the world. It is a public enterprise and Palmer is a public intellectual. But he brings a gift that is delivered through a unique language, a captivating and motivating language. Because of his approach, in many ways Palmer is making a more important contribution than the religious groups. Unlike many theorists in religious education, for example, whose work tends to be insular, reaching mostly a closed circle of like-minded people, Palmer's work on spirituality reaches across audiences, to the public and private sectors.

Linguistically, Palmer steps outside of what have become stale and sometimes offensive religious slogans, and instead he uses language that is re-imaginative and captivates the imagination of people. His awareness that some people have been hurt and disappointed by religious institutions, and have thus turned away from them, makes him cautious when he speaks of spiritual issues. His words, particularly in the latter years, are carefully crafted to steer clear of ecclesiastical language. Palmer captivated my imagination by seemingly stepping into my world and telling my story using a humane and thoughtful language. I could not put his books down and so I entered into his world and learned a whole new way of looking at myself as a teacher.

Given his gifts to engage many different people, Palmer can serve as a bridge between churches, mosques, and synagogues. He is also a link and a bridge between religious adherents, those who have no religious affiliation, and those who serve in the political arena. We have seen that, to reach such a variety of people and perspective, he deliberately learned to speak a second language—an alternative, secular language that has currency in the public square. To illustrate the adaptability of Palmer's work in various arenas, later in this chapter I introduce two of his mentees who are teachers outside of the conventional classroom, Greg Ellison II and Stephen Lewis.

Overall, this chapter synthesizes Palmer's philosophy of teaching and learning through his spiritual perspective with special attention to how his philosophy and spirituality contribute to the religious education practice in a classroom setting. As we have seen, among his many contributions is the work for which he is best known: his theory of living an authentic life. As he branched out to explore the dynamics of powerful leaders (Václav Havel, Rosa Parks, and Mahatma Gandhi), he noted that the effectiveness of these individuals was fueled by a passion that emerged from a deep-seated spirituality and a strong connection to the self.

An underlying element in this chapter is the distinctive pedagogical possibilities that religious educators are afforded because of the nature of their subject. Thomas Groome explains that fear of control by one religion created the separation of church and state in the United States. Unfortunately, the fear ultimately led to the development of an educational system completely devoid of spiritual influence.[2] This, in turn, has created a disconnect between what it means to form people's lives and what it means to educate them intellectually. Palmer calls this divide "our rigid separation of the visible world from the powers that undergird and animate it."[3] Religious educators have the advantage and responsibility of working to challenge this dichotomy.

As a teacher of religious studies in a Catholic high school in the United States, I enjoy the privilege, freedom, and responsibility to educate my students at the intersection of the spiritual and the intellectual. Palmer's theories of teaching, learning, and knowing have been valuable tools for informing and enriching my inner self and my work with students.

TEACHING GROUNDED IN PERSONHOOD AND COLLABORATIVE WORK

Palmer's perspectives add to the theories of religious education in several aspects. Chief among them is that he distinguishes himself from others in the field by focusing on the inner life of the teacher. While the educational system prizes tools and techniques for the classroom, Palmer views the teacher as the most valuable resource. He argues that the school teacher's inner life is what can determine success or failure in the classroom, a concept that is both profound and counter-cultural.

His conviction about the importance of leading an undivided life underscores all of his work, and is inseparably linked to his pedagogical theory. As such, Palmer's theory of education is deeply spiritual and profoundly humanistic. Of significance to the *religious* educator, specifically, is the emphasis he places on the *soul* of the teacher, that which animates

---

2. Groome, *Educating for Life*, 87.
3. Palmer, *To Know as We Are Known*, 10.

the human being. He advocates self-care: listening and responding to one's inner soul. In many ways, Palmer's work is an invitation to examine what we project, and why, when we teach religious subjects.

Palmer also addresses ways in which the academy can contribute towards the growth of the teacher, spiritually and professionally, or thwart that growth. In *The Courage to Teach*, he writes about the spirited new teachers who enter the profession with a vision and high expectations, but who become disillusioned and then burned-out and quickly abandon the profession.[4] The cause, says Palmer, is the culture of isolation that exists in the academy. In most schools, there is no community and little to no support for teachers.

To clarify, community in this context does not refer to groups of teachers who have become friends in and outside of the school. Community refers to the relationship that exists among and between the school's faculty members as a whole. Palmer maintains that working in community leads to learning and growing in one's craft alongside fellow teachers. Support needs to come from the administrators in the form of genuine care, attentiveness, and responsiveness to the needs of the teacher.

In addition to the lonely entry into the profession, other problems are prevalent in the academy. Palmer considers school teaching to be "perhaps the most privatized of all public professions."[5] He strengthens his point by contrasting the isolation of teaching with the work of other professions. For example, he notes that surgeons perform operations in a community of fellow surgeons whose support during the process keeps the patient alive. Having a team also guards the head surgeon from the possibility of a malpractice lawsuit.

To complicate matters further, the competitive nature of the academy discourages school teachers from discussing the problems they encounter. Instead, they are left alone either to figure things out or to berate themselves for being inept. Given the pitfalls of isolation and privatization, one can argue that teacher collaboration amongst religious educators should be the cornerstone of their practice. Religious educators are uniquely positioned to make this a reality because of the nature of one's mission, which parallels that of the church: to engage in dialogue with others, to demonstrate a level of listening that engages the heart as much as the mind, and to learn from one another.

4. Palmer, interview by author, Madison, Wisconsin, April 5, 2010.
5. Palmer, *Courage to Teach*, 146.

Despite the negative aspects of privatization, there are some who prefer it. As Palmer notes, it is unfortunate that teaching in isolation is often referred to as "academic freedom—my classroom is my castle."[6] Instead, he believes that privatization is a destructive element of teaching. For it is not possible to learn the craft of teaching without continuously observing others. To make matters worse for teachers, administrators generally ask students to evaluate the faculty based on a standardized questionnaire. This practice reduces the complex art of teaching to a few focal points, and responses (as in most optional surveys) focus on the highest and lowest points. Given their inadequate and irrelevant nature as true measures of a teacher's ability, student survey results often leave teachers feeling distanced, humiliated, and demoralized.[7]

Moreover, there is more than one reason why the academy uses teacher evaluations. Palmer maintains that evaluation data is useful in the academic "shell game."[8] If the administration wants to fire a teacher who received good student evaluations, they can trivialize the results by interpreting them as merely a measure of that teacher's popularity. If the administration wants to maintain a teacher with poor student evaluations, they can dismiss these same evaluations, arguing that the survey has no relevance to the scholarship or particular service that he or she offers the academy (or, more likely, their particular institution). Research substantiates Palmer's point that most schools use these surveys to mean what they want them to mean.[9] These actions weaken the morale in schools as well as the teacher's resolve to continue in the profession.

By contrast, the support that is encouraged through teacher collaboration serves the students, the institution and, most important for Palmer, the inner life of the teacher. Although this is a critical point, Palmer curiously does not offer a concrete explanation of what such collaboration might look like. As a teacher of religious studies, my own examples of collaboration include exchanging ideas that one gleans from liturgical experiences or scriptural readings, and noting effective ways in which to incorporate these ideas into lessons for students. One example is to use a theme of a parable, such as love your neighbor as yourself, or the theme of God's unconditional love, and connect the themes to a current event. This gives the students

6. Palmer, *Courage to Teach*, 147.
7. Palmer, *Courage to Teach*, 147.
8. Palmer, *Courage to Teach*, 147.
9. Salazar, "Interrogating Teacher Evaluation," 463–76.

the opportunity to reflect and discuss the message and its relevance to a particular moment in time. Another form of collaboration is to teach one another new forms of technology that can be effective in teaching religious studies. There are interactive computer-based programs designed to engage students with the lessons. For example, students can become engaged in listening, watching, writing, reflecting, and answering a few questions about the topic at hand. This activity could then lead to a broader classroom discussion.

In addition to this kind of sharing and collegiality, voicing concerns and problems that one experiences in the classroom or in the school as a whole is a powerful way to establish closer bonds with colleagues, and eliminate the sense of isolation that one can experience. This last point is perhaps the most important factor in providing teachers with the kind of support that helps to strengthen their inner lives, and helps to bridge the divide within.

The lack of community and support in the academy seems to have its seeds in the mysterious nature of teaching. Recall Gabriel Moran's words, that "There is very little written about the act of teaching. No one really seems to know much about it, including those who write books on education."[10] Although this has been the reality since the late 1800s, by 1948 the number of teachers in the United States was nearly one million. From a financial perspective, the calculation was clear for universities across the nation: "training teachers made financial sense whether there was something to teach them or not."[11]

This seems to tie in with the results of a recent study of national and international assessments of student achievement, which was reported in the New York Times. The study found that efforts to improve education in the United States are "disappointing."[12] Researchers point to the low levels of student achievement as evidence that teacher educators are not improving their programs "perhaps because they do not know how to make productive changes." Furthermore, a growing number of educational researchers have challenged the still existing notion that all of the knowledge needed to prepare effective classroom teachers can be found within the walls of universities and colleges.[13]

10. Moran, *Showing How*, 1.
11. Green, *Building A+ Better Teacher*, 27.
12. Goldstein, "School Reforms Fail to Lift U.S.," 1.
13. Floden et al., "A Nation at Risk," 1, 2.

As I have witnessed, regardless of a teacher's years of experience (or lack thereof), a typical introduction to a new class entails an administrator handing the teacher a course book. After that, it is generally up to the teacher to figure things out for the remainder of the year—a rude awakening for most teachers, and likely a losing proposition for both teacher and students since a lack of preparedness could not possibly yield the best possible experience for either.

Religious educators face an additional challenge to those presented by the institutions in which they teach: the lack of interest in religion among youth and young adults. This has contributed to the increase of religiously unaffiliated individuals in the U.S. that has been reported in the Pew Research studies. There are a number of factors at the center of this issue. Looking at the Catholic Church, in particular, Paul Lakeland writes that it "has lost a lot of its moral force within the secular culture." This is due in part to the sex-abuse scandal, "but an important secondary consideration is the failure of the teaching church to present Catholic belief in a credible and consistent manner that shows compassion and recognizes the complexity of many of the moral issues with which we struggle today."[14]

According to Lakeland, the Catholic Church of the 1950s in the United States looked like a pillar of strength and unity, yet its collapse was sudden and complete. Although the church has endured, as a practicing Catholic I have witnessed that participation in liturgical services has dramatically declined, especially the participation of the family as a unit. Another radical shift is the practice of attending reconciliation services, a Sacrament for which people once stood in long lines. This virtually disappeared after the 1950s. Lakeland argues that underneath the veneer of perfection was a restlessness brought on by a shift of values that ultimately placed greater emphasis on a materialistic vision that was making the American dream attainable "in the new middle-class affluence of the '50s."[15]

The efforts of the Catholic Church to correct "the drift into moral anonymity" are clearly evident in the Second Vatican Council's Pastoral Constitution on the Church in the Modern World (*Gaudium et Spes*).[16] In this document, the Catholic Church took an extraordinary turn in acknowledging its urgent need to engage with the world and to learn from it. *Gaudium et Spes* articulates "a whole understanding of the church as having

---

14. Lakeland, *Catholicism at the Crossroads*, 148.
15. Lakeland, *Catholicism at the Crossroads*, 148.
16. Lakeland, *Catholicism at the Crossroads*, 152.

responsibility to the entire world beyond the church." As Lakeland points out, "Vatican II thus put the Catholic Church in dialogue with the secular culture."[17]

Palmer's work speaks directly to this void in the church and in our culture. It is a call to engage in genuine, heartfelt conversation with the other. By virtue of the call to teach and model Christ through our work, Christian religious educators are uniquely positioned to have these kinds of dialogues. As Palmer would advise, the first step is to have these kinds of conversation with each other, and thereby to build trust and support and become a resource to one another. When teachers are supported, they feel valued for who they are and what they bring to the school. Palmer believes this kind of recognition leads them to become good teachers. He adds that in the absence of this kind of support, self-care is the critical element that makes a good teacher. He recommends that teachers find resources for spiritual care outside of the institutions in which they work as it is virtually impossible to find this within institutions. This holds true as well for those teaching in religiously affiliated schools.

As discussed in previous chapters, Palmer created such a resource for teachers: the series of spiritual retreats called circle of trust. To go on retreat generally means to step back, to cease activity, to withdraw, to take refuge in a safe place. The primary aim is renewal of the spirit. Given his interest and background in religion and spirituality, Palmer created what can be viewed as an oasis for religious educators. In circle of trust retreats, Palmer's focus is on building a community where teachers feel safe to express their doubts and fears. He creates a space in which each participant is met with empathy, compassion, and respect. The retreats are based on a Quaker practice in which individuals journey alone together, meaning that the experience takes place in a group setting. The setting which Palmer creates is a shared, safe, and sacred space, which is not unlike a religious setting. Although he has worked hard and successfully to reach a broad audience outside of the religious sphere and incorporated nonsectarian language in doing so, the essence of the work remains deeply grounded in religious beliefs, teachings, and practices.

The goal of these circle gatherings is to explore the mysteries of teaching with the same respect and professionalism that is accorded other professions. Palmer shares what his explorations have uncovered and what he believes creates a successful teacher:

17. Lakeland, *Catholicism at the Crossroads*, 153.

> To grow in our practice, we have two primary places to go: to the inner ground from which good teaching comes and to the community of fellow teachers from whom we can learn more about ourselves and our craft... Resources that could help us teach better are available from each other—if we could get access to them. Circle retreats provide both of these places to go.[18]

The experience and what is taught in circle retreats make them unique in three ways: grounded-ness, continuity, and nonviolent response. First, a key aspect of the success of circle retreats is their ability to keep the person engaged with the world and feeling more grounded in their work, during and after the retreat. Palmer recalls his own retreat experiences as follows:

> Early on my journey, I learned about the Monday morning letdown that often follows an uplifting weekend retreat. After soaring for two days, my spirit sank when I got back to work. Faced with the demands of life in the "real world," the inner progress I thought I had made seemed like an illusion, and the new self I thought I had found faded like a mirage.
>
> But now I understand that those letdowns were due only in part to the rigors of the workday world and my lack of spiritual stamina. The retreats I went on, though well intended, were setups for despair... A circle of trust does not take us to the mountaintop only to let us down. It puts us on the Möbius strip, where we never leave the ground. Time after time, I have heard participants say, "This is the first retreat I've attended that did not leave me feeling 'high.' Instead, I feel more grounded in myself and more at home in the world."[19]

The image of the Möbius strip (see chapter 1) provides a visual aid for the inward and outward continuous flow of energy that humans absorb and radiate. Palmer uses it to describe how one inwardly assimilates outer cues and messages. In turn, these become the conditioned responses one projects outwardly to the world. The inner work that is done in the retreats reminds us that "we are constantly co-creating the world, so we need not be victims of it."[20] As such, the aim in a circle of trust retreat is to have individuals return to their daily lives "better able to engage it in life-giving ways."[21]

18. Palmer, *Courage to Teach*, 146.
19. Palmer, *Hidden Wholeness*, 168.
20. Palmer, *Hidden Wholeness*, 168.
21. Palmer, *Hidden Wholeness*, 168.

The second unique aspect of the retreats is continuity. Most retreats end with the final session or meal, and participants scatter back to their worlds. By contrast, circle of trust retreats are offered seasonally, and the same groups are invited to meet repeatedly throughout the year. This builds trust and community amongst the participants, enabling them to continue the relationships outside the retreats. The idea of continuity, in my opinion, is crucial for one's inner and outer work. It would be ideal for religious educators to form a circle of trust to witness the effects of the experience on their personal and professional lives, as well as the impact that they could have on others.

Since 1994, circle retreats have grown in cities throughout the United States as well as internationally. And like his books on the spirituality of education, Palmer's retreats have become very popular outside religiously affiliated schools, because the Spirit is always at work making itself present when people are searching for Truth. One reason for the pluralistic appeal is that the retreats welcome the variety of religious traditions. Another reason, he finds, is a more basic explanation:

> Educators of all sorts are in real pain these days, and that pain has compelled them to explore unconventional resources. The teachers I meet have no illusions that education is "working." They know that students are often served poorly in the classroom, and that their own growth as teachers is not supported by the system . . . They are ready to look beyond technique for whatever guidance may come from spiritual traditions.[22]

The last reason to which Palmer points is one that I see as an invitation for us religious educators to bring our expertise in spiritual traditions to just such a circle experience. By virtue of their training in spirituality, religious educators already have a particular advantage, and this training and their presence can enhance others' experience of the circle. A circle experience can also offer religious educators the opportunity to exercise their responsibility to share their resources.

The third unique aspect of the circle experience is learning what Palmer identifies as a "third way" to respond in a violent world. Violence, in this instance, is non-physical. It means living in a spiritually violent world where often the integrity or self-hood of the person is destroyed. When this happens, the ancient, animal instinct inherent in each of us triggers a "fight or flight" response. Both responses stem from fear and are violent in

---

22. Palmer, *To Know as We Are Known*, x.

nature. But there is a "third way" of responding, one that is deeply spiritual. This third way offers a nonviolent response to the violence of the world by pledging "to act in every situation in ways that honor the soul."[23]

Religious educators have this response woven into their practice by the nature of the subject they address and often also by the way in which they themselves have been shaped by such religious practices. Yet teaching about how to be in the world is never effective, says Palmer, unless one has the capacity to be the exemplar. For example, in telling the New Testament story of the "Good Samaritan," Jesus illustrates what it means to love one's neighbor as one's self. Jesus portrays the good Samaritan as someone who has loving and caring qualities which emanate from within himself (Luke 10:27). In the Hebrew Scriptures book of Leviticus, God says, "You shall treat the alien who resides with you no differently than the natives born among you; you shall love the alien as yourself; for you too were once aliens in the land of Egypt. I, the LORD, am your God" (Lev 19:34).

In daily interactions with students, religious educators encounter situations that allow one to practice such nonviolent responses. Palmer shares a personal example of caring for the other as he himself would want to be cared for and showing compassion. He once had a student he refers to as "the student from hell."[24] Most teachers have experienced "the student from hell" at least once in their careers. As Palmer describes, the student acted inappropriately on many levels. He was a young man who sat slumped in his chair with nothing on his desk. He showed boredom and apathy every day in the classroom.

However, when Palmer found himself in conversation with the student, he began to understand the behavior. He discovered that the student lived with his father who berated him for going to college. His father wanted him to understand that college was yet another ploy to have people like them believe they could get ahead in the world, when in reality they never would. Though wanting an education, the young man lived with the internal conflict that his father might be right. His classroom demeanor had sent Palmer the wrong message. The student was not "brain-dead": he was filled with paralyzing doubt, fear, and confusion.[25]

This encounter gradually led Palmer to transform his pedagogy into a way of teaching that is grounded in personhood—the student's, as well as

---

23. Palmer, *Hidden Wholeness*, 170.
24. Palmer, *Courage to Teach*, 44.
25. Palmer, *Courage to Teach*, 44.

the teacher's. The story is explicitly meaningful for the religious educator because it highlights ways in which we can learn more about ourselves and about our subject matter through the students that we teach. The learning in this case involves the gradual embodiment of the subject one teaches. For instance, the process of transformation began when Palmer realized that an underlying fear was causing the student to behave as he did. He recognized the student as an example of his own theory: what we internalize is projected outwardly into the world (and oftentimes misinterpreted). "Do not be afraid" is one of the most frequently used phrases in the teachings of Jesus. Yet, fear seems to be the underlying cause of most human conflicts. What exacerbates conflict is the continual circle of fear that flows within, among, and between individuals.

Religious educators have abundant resources within their traditions that can be drawn upon to foster faith and trust, thus decreasing fear and the conflict it causes in favor of nonviolent responses. An example is using the teachings of Christ in specific stories, such as when he calmed the storm in Matt 8:23–27. The story serves as a metaphor about one's inner turmoil that could shed light on the need to strengthen one's faith and trust in God.

Palmer also discovered that his own hidden fears may have provoked the problem. His was a fear of judgment. He was "afraid of being judged" by his young students and of being open to ridicule.[26] Once he became aware of the mutual fearfulness that existed among him and his students, he changed his approach: "I try to teach to their fearful hearts, and when I am able to do so, their minds often come along as well."[27] This illustrates how the metaphor of the wounded healer suits Palmer. He experienced all that he writes about, as a student, then teacher, and on losing and regaining heart in the academy. The following section describes how he applies his experience and theories in the classroom.

CURRICULUM OF THE CLASSROOM: CREATING SACRED SPACE

Curriculum has been defined in many ways. One way of defining it is the purposes, content, activities, and organizations of the educational program.[28] As in this case, most meanings of curriculum apply to school

---

26. Palmer, *Courage to Teach*, 48.
27. Palmer, *Courage to Teach*, 47.
28. Walker and Soltis, *Curriculum and Aims*, 1.

settings, but refer to it as the curriculum of education. As Moran emphasizes, a curriculum of education refers to the interplay of a variety of life forms within education. He points to family, classroom, work, and leisure as educative forms. "There is no end to education," no termination point.[29]

Elliot Eisner notes that the word "curriculum" came from the Latin *currere*, which means "the course to be run."[30] This conjures up the image of obstacles to be overcome, of a program series with a beginning and end. Historically, schools have offered a course of studies which students were to complete satisfactorily. Schools have also served as institutions that differentiate and segregate the able from the less able by providing more rigorous examinations "that open or close doors to further schooling."[31] In other words, historically there have been schools that, for a higher tuition, offer both a curriculum and examinations of "higher standards" to those who can afford a better education, thereby distinguishing the elite from the rest of the population. This remains true in the present.

As Eisner indicates, progressive educators in the 1920s did much to enhance the meaning of curriculum. They began by emphasizing the importance of experience. Although planning is important, for the progressive educators, "the real curriculum for the child, the one that made a difference in his or her life, was the curriculum that he or she experienced."[32] They also recognized the relevance of each child's uniqueness in their interests, backgrounds, and aptitudes. These factors contributed to their understanding that the curriculum is never the same for different children. A further point which he uncovered broadened the meaning of the curriculum of experience. Eisner writes: "To their credit, these same progressive educators recognized that what children learn in school is wider than what goes on in classrooms and more varied than what teachers intend to teach."[33] For example, students learn about the hidden curriculum where affluent students receive better accommodations than those with little resources.

Palmer begins the discussion of curriculum with the curriculum of community, and further develops it to include topics such as creating sacred space, uncovering or proclaiming truths, and the curriculum of service. He centers the curriculum of the classroom on the purpose of self-actualization.

---

29. Moran, *Showing How*, 156.
30. Eisner, *Educational Imagination*, 25.
31. Eisner, *Educational Imagination*, 26.
32. Eisner, *Educational Imagination*, 26.
33. Eisner, *Educational Imagination*, 26.

This can be accomplished only through relational experiences. To achieve the purpose, careful structuring of the environment is of the essence. It calls forth a teaching approach that is caring, human, and humanistic. The relational aspect of Palmer's approach to teaching is grounded in spirituality and invokes the divine energy that motivates individuals to open their hearts to one another. It calls for a classroom curriculum that is interwoven with the curriculum of community. In Palmer's pedagogical approach, he understands that community is what people most yearn for but find difficult to attain.

True to Palmer's calling is his political savvy about what schools are supposed to accomplish. His vision is fueled by the possibilities of human potential through learning. As Dwayne Huebner confirms, "Schooling has always been political. It always has been; it always will be."[34] Within the curriculum of the school is the curriculum of becoming socialized—learning to live as a society. This is the essence of what it means to be a religious educator: to teach one's students that the religious principles that one cherishes guide one's behavior and flow from one into the world, affecting society as a whole.

Huebner notes, "When schools were established they were seen as having a role in the maintenance of liberty . . . Dissemination of knowledge and information was assumed necessary to maintain government by free people, and to continue to be a free people."[35] Palmer views schooling as fertile ground for freedom. However, his vision of freedom is of a different kind—the freedom to be who we are called to be as individuals, within community. For him, this is the genesis of social transformation and it can begin with religious instruction.

The idea behind Palmer's theory of living an undivided life is symbiotic in nature. For example, he believes that if people truly honor who they are as spiritual, carnal, and interdependent beings made in the image of God, then it follows that in living one's deepest truth people will, in turn, honor the truth of those around them. This concept is a precursor to social change because it speaks to who and how we are called to be as a people of God. As religious educators will note, although in this world it is a highly idealistic concept, Palmer's theory about authenticity, living one's truth, or living undividedly as he words it, is a message that permeates biblical Scripture and is highlighted in the New Testament. The acceptance of yourself

---

34. Huebner, "Curriculum . . . With Liberty and Justice for All," 1.
35. Huebner, "Curriculum . . . With Liberty and Justice for All," 2.

and of your fellow human would usher in a more peaceful and equitable world. Palmer's thought follows several golden rules: "Do unto others as you would have done unto you," Jesus' words, "Love one another as I have loved you," and "Love your neighbor as yourself."

Having discovered that the key to achieving our human potential lies in our ability to learn how to live integrated lives, Palmer turned his attention towards helping others realize this. His practice is centered on teaching to the hearts and minds of his students. He believes this practice leads to recognition and respect for individuality and thus honors the student's true identity. He firmly believes that schools (and I would add classes in religious studies) could be a place where the inner self is nurtured.

For Palmer, teachers need to come from a place of love in their hearts in order to reach students at their heart's core. Many students are looking for a place like this. Dwayne Huebner writes that most of us assume the home is the place where love can be found but not in institutions, especially not in schools—and for good reason. He notes, "The careless structures of our society appear to have become dominant in schools and other formal places of education."[36] Schools have become places where the underscored aim is competition and advancement.

Adding to the complexity of human interactions and the search for love is William Pinar's observation that family is not "a haven in a heartless world (Lasch 1977): it is a complex, if singular, configuration of that world."[37] This last point underscores the need for religious educators in schools to become humanistic in their approach to students, as the subject of religion lends itself most readily to have a broad, positive impact in the institutions they serve. Palmer argues for schools to take on this task in order to become the place that students are looking for: a place where they can be themselves, be heard, be understood, and feel acceptance. From Palmer's perspective, schools could become the place that students can call home in a heartless world, and I see the potential for religious studies faculty to make that become a reality. The elements that Palmer and others list as necessary to achieve this kind of school environment underscore this. Each element directly references religious studies.

As Palmer notes, the academy has become a heartless world because the sacred has been driven out of it. While Palmer emphasizes the fear that

---

36. Huebner, "Religious Metaphors," 364.

37. Pinar, *Race, Religion, and a Curriculum of Reparation*, 5; quoting Lasch, *Culture of Narcissism*.

permeates the academy (fear of judgment, fear of ridicule, fear of being labeled incompetent, etc.), Huebner writes of a lack of love in the academy. As Palmer affirms, self-care and leading an authentic life enable a teacher to develop their gifts in such a complex and conflict-driven environment. However, there is another component for which he recognizes the need. In the process of exploring ways to reach his students, Palmer came to this conclusion: the classroom needs to be regarded as sacred space. This conviction bears particular relevance for religious educators.

A re-constructed and re-imaginative vision of schooling is necessary in order to regard teaching as a sacramental act, and the classroom as sacred space. The prototypical view of education is that of one person exercising power over others. This extends to the classroom. Beginning in elementary school, students are taught that their most important task is to learn the single correct answer to each question: answers that the teacher knows and the students need to learn.[38] According to Gabriel Moran, "Teaching becomes confused with a certain arrangement of power (one of great inequality); in addition, the coercive influence is exercised mainly or exclusively through words."[39] He argues that unless teaching is framed in a larger, wider context, it can become a negative experience where students are kept "dutifully servile."[40]

As Eisner notes, it is difficult to change the culture of schools. Schools have a long history of emphasizing hard work and undervaluing imagination, the human spirit, and creative thinking.[41] As this section illustrates, Palmer's practice in the classroom space lends itself to the interplay of forms. As Palmer notes and as I have discussed previously, the dynamics of three variables are at play in the classroom—the teacher, the students, and the subject. The subject itself has a voice.[42]

Palmer's pedagogical theory is articulated as six paradoxes, which I summarized in chapter 3.[43] Rooted in spirituality, each offers valuable insights for the religious educator. The first paradox: that the teaching space should be both bounded and open. Bounded refers to a structure that is established, where the student's attention is drawn to a focal point. This

---

38. Eisner, *Educational Imagination*, 55.
39. Moran, *Religious Education as a Second Language*, 63.
40. Moran, *Religious Education as a Second Language*, 64.
41. Eisner, *Educational Imagination*, 55.
42. Palmer, *To Know as We Are Known*, 98.
43. Palmer, *Courage to Teach*, 76.

could be accomplished in a number of ways: by using a text, a quotation, or perhaps a question. A religious studies class could easily begin with a question to form the structure of the conversation to follow. Palmer notes that this method has been used by the greatest teachers: "Teaching by questioning was the genius of Socrates, of Jesus, and of the desert father, Abba Felix."[44] As a boundary, the question provides students with clarity about what is expected and how the class will proceed. If boundaries are not set, a classroom can become chaotic. However, its opposite, openness, provides the space for new discoveries to be made, for "the surprises that always come with real learning."[45]

Palmer's second paradox is: "the space should be hospitable and charged."[46] In such a space, students feel welcome and safe. More important, they should be made to feel that they matter. A hospitable space encourages students to open their hearts and minds. Jesus always taught by making reference to issues, experiences, or things to which people could easily relate. Religion offers the unique opportunity to engage students in topics that most interest them, by connecting people's greatest interests with the religious tradition. In this case, the topic itself could be what charges the space. A charged space invites students to think and challenges them to respond. In such a space, students are not inclined to withdraw into their own world.

Students want to be heard and will often engage in dialogue when given the space to do so. Palmer recognizes this opportunity in the third paradox: "the space should invite the voice of the individual and the voice of the group."[47] This illustrates the importance of feeling that one is in a communal environment where there is trust. Palmer creates this space by teaching his students the value of their individual insights. He also emphasizes the value of listening and hearing what others have to say.

The fourth paradox broadens the concept of listening and speaking: "the space should honor the 'little' stories of the students and the 'big' stories of the disciplines and traditions."[48] This is where a religious studies teacher could draw the connection between what is shared and what scripture teaches one. This kind of space allows for deeper reflection as one

---

44. Palmer, *To Know as We Are Known*, 82.
45. Palmer, *Courage to Teach*, 77.
46. Palmer, *Courage to Teach*, 77.
47. Palmer, *Courage to Teach*, 78.
48. Palmer, *Courage to Teach*, 79.

listens to what the individual and the subject have to say. While the subject can speak to student experiences and inform their lives, the student's personal realities help further the understanding of the subject matter.

However, while communal learning is important, at the same time learning requires time alone to reflect. Palmer's fifth paradox thus consists of community and solitude. Solitude provides the space for the inner teacher to surface. He asserts, only in solitude can the inner teacher be heard.[49] The practice of prayer and meditation in a religion class can be a form of teaching how to access one's inner teacher, or the guidance of the Holy Spirit.

Palmer's sixth paradox addresses the two opposite poles of reflection and speaking: "the space should welcome both silence and speech."[50] While he encourages his students to voice their thoughts, he is also aware of the student's right not to speak. He has found that giving students this right creates another interesting paradox: the safety of this space actually invites the student to speak. As a religious studies teacher, I am aware of how the Spirit could be working among the students, regardless of whether they say anything in class. Sometimes what a student receives is not for sharing, while at other times they may be prompted to speak.

Beyond the insights expressed through his six paradoxes, Palmer's theory of pedagogy adds various dimensions to the classroom experience. He does not limit the classroom experience to the cognitive level of learning and knowing, or to the objective mode of knowing things at a distance. He deepens the learning experience by tapping into multiple senses. Here his theory addresses the religious aspects of teaching. According to Palmer, the self is above all communal, and it calls us into relationship with others and with truths to be known.[51] His overarching framework is an approach which holds that in faith, and together, he and his students will uncover truths. His aim is to establish a space where students are immersed in a relationship that involves the self as much as it does the other—the "other" meaning the subject along with the other people who are co-learners.

These relationships form the curriculum of community in the school classroom and are particularly relevant to religious education in a number of ways. For example, the concept of living in community and discovering in relation to one another and to the world around us undergirds Catholic

---

49. Palmer, *Courage to Teach*, 79.
50. Palmer, *Courage to Teach*, 80.
51. Palmer, *To Know as We Are Known*, 53.

social teaching. Furthermore, the exploration of the incomprehensible and omnipotent aspects of God can only take place as a cohesive body of people who trust one another, share common beliefs, practices, and the desire to understand their religious tradition more fully. The concept of relational learning and dimensions relevant for religious education I examine further in the following section.

Included is the work of Palmer's mentee, Greg Ellison, mentioned earlier in chapter 1, which provides insights into forming relationships of truth and creating a curriculum of community. It also shows how Palmer influenced Ellison in his teaching and in his search to form relationships of truth. Though Ellison does not teach in a conventional classroom setting, the concepts and tools that he employs can be readily adapted to a classroom environment.

CURRICULUM OF COMMUNITY: TRUTH AS REVEALED IN THE NATURE OF KNOWLEDGE

The communal tradition of Christianity informs what might be regarded as Palmer's idea of a curriculum of community within a school setting. He articulates this Christian value in a discourse on epistemology, where he uncovers four concepts about truth: "truth is personal, truth is communal, truth is reciprocal, and truth is transformational."[52] Together, they form the framework for his theory of teaching and learning in community. He states: "I do not believe that epistemology is a bloodless abstraction. The way we know has powerful implications for the way we live. There is a link between epistemology and life."[53] Palmer notes that these concepts "might move us toward a transformed understanding of knowing."

For the religious educator, the ideas are significant because the way in which students come to know their truth will determine how they live out their lives in the world. In other words, are one's truths exclusive to oneself, or does one apply them to others? The answer reveals how this person is in the world. The concept of truth as personal runs counter to modern objectivism, where truth is viewed as something apart from us that needs to be pursued. Palmer views truth through the lens of Christianity where truth and personhood are inextricably linked—personal, incarnate, and real. For example, Jesus revealed this when he was asked, "What is truth?"

52. Palmer, "Violence of Our Knowledge," 10.
53. Palmer, *Seeking Vocation*, 2.

and he responded by stating, "'I AM . . . the truth.'"[54] Truth as personal and incarnate is confirmed in John 1:14:

> And the Word became flesh
> and made his dwelling among us . . .
> full of grace and truth.

Palmer interprets truth as personal, as the human call to speak and live honestly "in an effort to embody the truth as we know it."[55]

Envisioning truth as communal is "a statement that you are person only in community."[56] It refers to truth as that which emerges in a shared discourse about the questions of life. Palmer views the classroom as a space where truth can be cultivated. Another way in which he explains this concept is that a "community of truth" is "a rich and complex network of relationships in which we must both speak and listen, make claims on others, and make ourselves accountable."[57] This theory holds that there can never be a truth for some but not for others, a notion that is having a destructively polarizing effect in our contemporary society. Truth can only be communal.

Truth as reciprocal is the spiritual understanding that as we seek truth, truth also seeks us. Palmer offers Einstein as an example of someone who devoted nearly a lifetime to "'listening to the universe speak.'"[58] His view of the universe was not of an object to be known. For Einstein, the universe was the knowing, the truth—that which spoke to him as the knower. According to Palmer, when we regard truth as personal, communal, and reciprocal, we are inevitably transformed by it.

Hospitality is the key element in the curriculum of community.[59] Only in a hospitable environment can such complicated conversations take place and yield a positive outcome. The transformation is more likely to occur in a safe environment, where one is able to discern who the other person is with the depth of understanding that Palmer delineates as truth. The revelation can change the dynamics of how one relates to humankind. A model of how one can develop such spaces is demonstrated in the work of Greg Ellison. I interviewed Ellison to show how he implemented Palmer's

---

54. Palmer, "Violence of Our Knowledge," 11.
55. Palmer, "Violence of Our Knowledge," 11.
56. Palmer, "Violence of Our Knowledge," 11.
57. Palmer, *To Know as We Are Known*, xii.
58. Palmer, "Violence of Our Knowledge," 12.
59 Palmer, *Courage to Teach*, 78.

theories to create a safe space to have difficult conversations. Learning truths that will last a lifetime is the goal of the programs he developed as founder of Fearless Dialogue. Although Ellison does not teach in a classroom setting, his pedagogical approach is easily adaptable to the traditional school classroom.

In 2013, Gregory Ellison II founded Fearless Dialogues, a grassroots organization that creates unique spaces for unlikely partners to engage in difficult, heartfelt conversations. As I wrote in chapter 1, upon meeting, Ellison and Palmer discovered that their grandfathers actually knew and respected one another. This shared history created a rather unique bond between them. It became quite evident in my interview with Ellison that he has a deep affection for Palmer. There were moments when he became emotional as he articulated what Palmer has meant to him on various levels.

Over the years, Palmer became Ellison's "theoretical interlocutor, mentor, vocational guide, spiritual sojourner, and friend." Ellison states that he has also been deeply informed by Palmer's research and credits his book *The Company of Strangers* as foundational to the work that he does at Fearless Dialogues, because essential to engaging unlikely partners in conversation is the wisdom of knowing how to rise above one's fear of strangers. Ellison has adapted Palmer's theories for groups rather than individuals and has applied them with the goal of moving people into action for personal and social transformation.

The methodology of Fearless Dialogues is built upon the framework of the Quaker practice of Clearness Committees and Palmer's derivation of it. Fearless Dialogues is also guided by three pillars: See, Hear, and Change. For if one cannot see another individual, with whom one disagrees, as a whole human being made in the image and likeness of God, it is not possible for one to hear as meaningful anything that the person has to say. Says Ellison, "If you cannot see or hear them, any change that is created will not be sustainable. What our work is built on is helping people to see that which most people overlook and to hear those things that others might ignore."

A college student orientation provides an example of how the organization has applied this in a school setting. The orientation served as a space in which the students were led to a heightened awareness of the environment they were entering into so that they could learn to see the people who do not agree with them and still be able to hear them. Ellison and his colleagues at Fearless Dialogues are continually innovating to create a malleable pedagogy that is interactive and seeks to deal with different learning styles. Their experiments, which are applicable for a variety of institutions, are interactive and involve movement. For example, Ellison engages his participants in a variety of media forms including art and music and leads them in large and small group conversations.

Another strategy that Ellison implements in his institutional work is a series of experiments that enables him to create a safe, hospitable environment—a *container*. Among the many experiments that Ellison has held in this container is one where the participants (who are employees of an institution at various different levels and job titles) are asked to choose a gift badge instead of a name tag as they enter the space. The selection of gifts to choose from on these badges are: activist, artist, educator, healer, anchor, or connecter. By choosing a gift badge Ellison explains that a person is staking a claim that "This is a gift that I identify from my soul." This is a way in which his work seeks to decenter power and hierarchies in Fearless Dialogues workshops. The purpose as he explains it is "so that unlikely partners who might not ordinarily speak, are now sitting in close proximity to each other and talking about their affinities, their gifts and things that enliven their souls as opposed to their roles and titles, which could be divisive." Palmer's language is evident throughout this work. Woven throughout Ellison's work are also adaptations of the work of his other vocational and spiritual guides, which include poet Mari Evans, Barbara Brown Taylor, and Luther Smith.[60]

Palmer wrote the foreword to Ellison's book titled *Fearless Dialogues: A New Movement for Justice*. It was published in 2017. In 2018 I had the privilege of partaking in a Fearless Dialogue presentation at a Religious Education Association conference outside Washington, DC. The energy in the room was heightened by Ellison's dynamic personality and the innovative use of gift badges. I was able to witness the power of that concept at work among individuals who at first seemed to be unlikely partners to engage in conversation. Palmer would have been proud of the work he has influenced and inspired. The synergy in their work has been brought to the public arena. Ellison shared with me that he and Palmer have made a number of presentations together. Viewed from their own lens, Palmer and Ellison are unlikely partners who one day came together on a back porch to converse about their shared vision. Little did they know just how much they had in common.

---

60. Ellison, interview by author, video conference, May 11, 2019.

Of importance to the field of religious education is to create in the classroom such a *container* or hospitable space. Only in such a safe space can complicated issues be approached, examined, and pondered. Palmer's view about hospitality is that it is "a virtue central to the biblical tradition itself, where God is always using the stranger to introduce us to the strangeness of truth. To be inhospitable to strangers or strange ideas, however unsettling they may be, is to be hostile to the possibility of truth; hospitality is not only an ethical virtue but an epistemological one as well."[61]

Dwayne Huebner reinforces this prioritization of hospitality. Influenced by Palmer's work in *The Company of Strangers*, Huebner writes that love enables us to acknowledge the stranger in our midst. He adds, "Thus education is a call from the other that we may reach out beyond ourselves and enter into life with the life around us."[62]

For Palmer, a space must also be one "in which obedience to truth is practiced."[63] He notes that outside of a religious context, obedience is a word that carries negative connotations. However, the hermeneutic he applies is its fuller, deeper meaning. He writes, "it means to listen with a discerning ear and respond faithfully to the personal implications of what one has heard. Obedience does not mean slavish, mechanical adherence to whatever one hears; it means making a personal response that acknowledges that one is in troth with the speaker and with the words he or she speaks."[64]

This has significance for religious education in that Palmer uncovers the true meaning of a word that most students find problematic. He also addresses a practice that has turned people away from religion. In previous generations, and still today, one was taught to obey God and religious teachings without questioning. Thomas Merton understood the importance of questioning one's religion, noting that "You cannot be a [person] of faith unless you know how to doubt. You cannot believe in God unless you are capable of questioning the authority of prejudice, even though that prejudice may seem to be religious."[65] When understood in the context in which Palmer explains it, the word "obedience" becomes a term of usefulness and importance. Palmer's focus in writing and teaching is to apply the

---

61. Palmer, *To Know as We Are Known*, 74.
62. Huebner, "Religious Metaphors," 360.
63. Palmer, *To Know as We Are Known*, 88.
64. Palmer, *To Know as We Are Known*, 89.
65. Merton, *New Seeds of Contemplation*, 105.

rule of truth: "A rule that can order our inquiries and bring us all, knowers and known, into mutually obedient relationships of truth."[66] Entering into the reality of the other is the cornerstone of the curriculum of, and the practice of, communal living.

Stephen Lewis has devoted much of his career to communal work. Developing the skills of his students to listen with a discerning ear and to respond faithfully has been a focus in his work. The goal of Lewis's organization is to empower ministers to be of service to their community. I interviewed Lewis to show how Palmer influenced him, and how he adapted Palmer's theories for his teaching environment. As the following demonstrates, both Palmer and Lewis have developed theories that can contribute to a curriculum of service in a school setting.

CURRICULUM OF SERVICE FOR EMPOWERMENT— "CHANNELING POWER IN A HUMAN FORM"

Stephen Lewis is President of the Forum for Theological Exploration (FTE), an organization founded in 1954 to nurture quality and diverse leadership for Christian ministry and theological scholarship. At the start of my interview with Lewis he explained that his organization was doing Clearness Committee work, which is a three-hundred-year-old Quaker-based practice, long before he ever met Palmer. What drew him to Palmer's work was the connection between their work centering around spirituality, leadership, and vocation. Key to what he uncovered was the "brilliance of [Palmer] having codified methodically a set of practices and processes that help give deeper speech to people's own kind of inner dialogue in soul and role."[67] Lewis was aware of a five-page document that Palmer had created, which outlined the purpose and method of a Clearness Committee. A colleague of his had implemented Palmer's five-page document into the work at FTE.

Lewis read more of Palmer's work and eventually reached out to him by phone. He explained what he saw as synergistic qualities in their work and expressed an interest in knowing more about Palmer's work. Palmer invited Lewis and his colleagues to his home in Wisconsin for a conversation

---

66. Palmer, *To Know as We Are Known*, 89.

67. Lewis, interview by author, video conference, June 9, 2019. All subsequent quotes by Lewis are from this interview.

on his back porch. A working relationship was soon established and both men set out to look at ways in which to build young leaders.

The catalyst to explore Palmer's work further came when FTE was trying to figure out how to lead change. As Lewis explains it, there is a need within society and in church-related organizations to move away from living divided and to form communities of congruence. To that end he was "trying to start a signature leadership program for young persons of color who were trying to figure out how to lead change in their organizational context. This became a project called Project Rising Sun." It was based on a theory that Lewis was working on that said that "The quality of one's community engagement is inextricably tied to their capacity to build their own institutions or their own organizational capacity. And one's ability to do that well is inextricably tied to their own personal formation."

Palmer's theories began to shed further light on some of the things that Lewis was trying to accomplish. This led him to modify parts of the work to achieve his goals with FTE. For example, Lewis viewed Clearness Committees as essential for personal growth. However, he noted that the way in which Palmer used this tool left the individual with no accountability about what they are going to do with what they had become clear about. He stated as an example that "People can get clear about their New Year's resolution and not act on it." For Lewis, this was a logical next step in helping the individual and the missing piece in Palmer's work.

After discovering this factor, FTE began to work on the question: "How do you get clear about something and then begin prototyping it and embodying it in your organization and in your life?" This was a powerful realization and one that fit perfectly with taking FTE to a new level of leadership development. In other words, Lewis wanted to challenge his students to at least take small steps, "their most faithful step in what it is that they have discerned [about] what they have been called to." For Lewis the importance of this next step in forming new leaders after they reached clarity about their vocation was summarized in his favorite quote from Howard Thurman: "Don't ask yourself what the world needs. Ask yourself what makes you come alive, and go do that, because what the world needs is people who have come alive." Clearness Committees are still used at FTE, but they are integrated with other practices to help the students think about their next step in their role as ministers who can be active participants and co-creators of a future that we all long to see.

Lewis also differs from Palmer in the discernment process. Palmer focuses on individual discernment, and Lewis has adapted the process for communal discernment, focusing on the whole community of leaders that he is training, versus one individual. He believes that our pressing problems require the kind of collective wisdom of the whole in order to come up with better solutions for an alternative future. Lewis asks the question: "Who is the smartest person in the room?" And he responds with: "It is not one individual, but it is the room itself."

Lewis also holds a different view about the importance of silence. While he understands the value of silence for discernment, he explained to Palmer that "for those of us who are people of color whose voices have been silenced in this country, silence is not the only option [for discernment] nor is it important. We know people who access their inner knowing or spirit through gospel music and other ways." A question that he asks his students in the discernment process is: "Can you get still enough? Not just quiet enough, but still enough to hear the unique rumbling within yourself to hear the sound of the genuine."

This led Lewis to also explore Palmer's retreats to see what he could glean and modify for his purposes at FTE. In the process, he became one of Palmer's retreat leaders for two years. The "codified process of bringing people together in level sets where people have different levels of power and different levels of agency" was what intrigued Lewis the most. Level sets refers to a method of decentering power where people who would be unlikely to mingle are brought together in conversation. Ellison's example of using gift badges to accomplish this is a prime example of the "level set" concept. It brings individuals to the same level where they share common ground. Through his studies and experiences Lewis brought a new process to FTE called C.A.R.E., an acronym that stands for Creating space, Asking self-awakening questions, Reflecting theologically, and Enacting one's next most faithful step.

Overall, in creating the framework for FTE's work with young leaders, Lewis adapted some of the work from various sources, which included Juanita Brown, Meg Wheatley, and Parker Palmer. In general, Lewis sees FTE as "more of a hybrid between Palmer's circle of trust retreats and the Theory U model by Otto Scharmer," who wrote the 2018 publication *The Essentials of Theory U: Core Principles and Applications*.

At the time of this interview, Lewis and his colleagues, Matthew Wesley Williams and Dori Grinenko Baker, were working on a book titled

Another Way: Living and Leading Change on Purpose, and Palmer was writing the foreword. The book was published in 2020. It was born out of the co-authors' belief that there has to be another way to create safe spaces, to arrive at vocational discernment, and to sustain people of faith who want to lead change and break through a system of power and privilege. In the opening reviews of the book, Richard Rohr describes this book as follows: "Here you will find a way of reengaging the Way of Jesus and exploring what that means, both at a personal and organizational level."[68]

The spiritual and humanistic approach is the common thread that runs throughout the work of Lewis and Palmer. Together they have inspired many young leaders to go out into the world and effect change through the work of their respective organizations. Overall, Lewis and Ellison are examples of the many leaders that Palmer has helped to shape. In his conversations with Palmer, Lewis became aware that Palmer was interested in meeting more young writers, activists, and teachers with whom he could share some of the strategies that he had developed over the years, and it was he who introduced Greg Ellison to Palmer.

The idea of reclaiming one's own power, as well as creative engagement between self and the world for service and empowerment of others anchor Palmer's theories. Stephen Lewis developed this theory to focuses on empowering individual ministers in ways that, in turn, empower communities. Of significance for religious educators is that, in the context of school, Palmer's theories and practices, as well the theories and practices of those whom he has mentored, provide a model of diverse forms of education which point to the central message of Jesus—love one another. Palmer's approach aims to empower individuals, who in turn can help empower a community. His model not only encompasses Jesus' compassionate, nonviolent approach for social change, but also adheres to the proverb which states, "Give a man a fish and you feed him for a day. Teach a man to fish and you feed him for a lifetime."

Developing change that can feed communities for a lifetime has been the focus of the two organizations run by Gregory Ellison II and Stephen Lewis. Their work has not only been influenced by Parker Palmer, but they both enjoy a personal relationship with him and with each other. As Palmer noted in my last interview with him, the work of Lewis and Ellison stands apart from what he does in his organization, *The Center for Courage & Renewal*. He explained that, in their work, Lewis and Ellison set out to move

---

68. Lewis et al., *Another Way Is Possible,* front matter.

individuals into action, whereas Palmer's work focuses on the interior of the individual.

Palmer commented that "the work of Lewis and Ellison is complementary, not competitive to *Courage* work in that they are looking to take people in a direction, whereas *Courage* work prepares people to enter brave spaces. This work frees people to figure out where they stand. *Courage* work is not designed to take people where we want people to go."[69] While each of these organizations is unique, the way in which they operate can be distinguished from *Courage* work is that Lewis and Ellison develop Palmer's work in vital directions beyond personal transformation toward organizational change to address deep-seated injustices in society.

The stories of Palmer, Lewis, and Ellison show how much common ground they share. First, they each acknowledged the call to work towards uncovering the self. Secondly, they were each motivated to work towards healing the racial divide in our country. And thirdly, the message of love underscores their work. Palmer's vocation began early in his life. It formally started in 1969 when he completed his doctorate degree on the sociology of religion and began to look for ways to apply his knowledge.

As he recalls, he was eager to go out into the world and "do sociology" rather than intellectualize about it.[70] His first job was on a community project which focused on the creative potential of racial diversity. His focus during those years was on involving the college students in his community service work. He used an experiential approach as a way of teaching and learning for transformation. This was, and remains, at the center of his teaching practice, which is an integrated and holistic approach. It mirrors his inner spirituality and deep-seated belief in the power of love. He aims to integrate self-love with communal love, so as to transform, without any use of violence in words or deeds, the way one lives in the world. He absorbed this understanding and the importance of blending curricula (classroom, community, and service) through his own personal sojourn.

The experiences at Pendle Hill, and its multiple curricula, are woven into Palmer's pedagogy and discourses as a public intellectual. There is virtually no distinction between his approach and message, whether he is in the public sphere or the classroom. Connecting to our spirituality and serving one another are the themes that undergird all of his work. For example, he advocates the gospel of abundance. He notes, "Scarcity and abundance

---

69. Palmer, interview by author, telephone call, April 29, 2019.
70. Intrator, *Living the Questions*, xxxiii.

are fundamental concepts in the political and economic travail of our times. The world is split into 'haves' and 'have-nots.'"[71] He postulates that there is a connection among scarcity, abundance, and our spiritual lives. But this connection has not been understood to the point where we can properly "respond to political and economic wrongs."[72] Correcting the imbalances in the world has always been a primary concern for him.

Matthew Fox, an American Episcopal priest and theologian, holds a similar view to Palmer's on human spirituality and the injustices in the world. Fox draws on a rich legacy of great mystics and philosophers from the East and West in his book entitled *The Reinvention of Work*, which includes insights from master thinkers such as Meister Eckhart, Thomas Aquinas, and the writers of *Bhagavad Gita* and *Tao Te Ching*. He makes an insightful point: "An authentic spirituality of work will address unemployment. It is telling that people who live in a cosmology do not have unemployment. There was no unemployment among native peoples."[73] By "living in a cosmology," Fox is referring to societies where people live according to the natural laws of the universe from the time of creation.

To explain his position further, Fox quotes Marshall Sahlins: "'The world's most primitive people have few possessions, but they are not poor. Poverty is not a certain amount of goods, nor is it just a relation between means and ends; above all it is a relation between people. Poverty is a social status. As such it is the invention of civilization.'"[74] I agree with Sahlins's finding and argue that the Western contemporary cosmology that we live in is a society that is ordered around an individualistic ideology. In this worldview, people outside of one's intimate circle are kept at a guarded distance, lest there be intimacy between strangers. Such divisions foster lack of care for those who are not our intimates and they perpetuate inequalities.

Complementing Fox's viewpoint, Palmer notes, "If our inner life is one of scarcity, and grasping, we will surely not live an outward witness to a just and merciful sharing of the earth's goods."[75] For Palmer, scarcity and abundance are aspects of the human spiritual quest. He suggests three ways to help us move towards our true human, life-affirming instincts: through education, community, and prayer. By prayer, he refers to "a life

---

71. Palmer, *Promise of Paradox*, 94.
72. Palmer, *Promise of Paradox*, 94.
73. Fox, *Reinvention of Work*, 134.
74. Fox, *Reinvention of Work*, 135.
75. Palmer, *Promise of Paradox*, 95.

that returns constantly to that silent, solitary place within us where we encounter God and life's abundance becomes manifest."[76] As noted earlier, these life-affirming elements are articulated in his pedagogical theory and practiced as interplay of curricula.

Among those who follow this principle are Jesuit high schools, such as the one where I teach. The mission of these schools, founded in fidelity to the vision of St. Ignatius of Loyola, is to educate students to be spiritually motivated, intellectually accomplished, and committed to promoting social justice. The ideology which undergirds the schools' curricula is that of Catholic social teaching and the Ignatian motto of forming "Men and women for others."

Within the Ignatian tradition and others like it, Catholic social teaching refers to connecting with one's humanness by uncovering one's spirituality. It emphasizes learning about who one is in the context of the other, and understanding one's interdependence with the other by reaching out to the poor, the oppressed, and the marginalized. In short, Catholic social teaching is about one's identity as Christian, one's relationship to the world, and one's faith as disciples of Christ. The practice of service "conserves" this Christian tradition. Dwayne Huebner writes: "Education as conservation seems strange."[77] However, he notes that the overall purpose of education is to conserve knowledge of great importance in the collective memory of the people.

The Christian tradition of service is greatly valued among Catholic schools. Service includes projects ranging from students working at homeless shelters, nursing homes, and schools for underprivileged students, to home constructions projects for the poor. Also included is travel to allegedly under-resourced countries where students experience first-hand what life in those settings is like. Fund-raising and advocacy campaigns for particular causes are other forms of service. Advocacy campaigns generally center around influencing changes in government policy on current, pressing issues.

Service projects enable students to grow spiritually. The experiential approach often leads to conversion of heart. The students gain awareness and a different perspective when they witness the life and struggles of another. They come to understand that the heart cannot feel what the eyes do not see. They also learn the importance of getting others involved in

---

76. Palmer, *Promise of Paradox*, 114.
77. Huebner, "Curriculum ... With Liberty and Justice for All," 6.

the service. They learn about the world in ways that classroom teaching cannot provide. In the process, the students also make a number of self-discoveries, which include revelations about their own talents and gifts or about their beliefs, assumptions, and knowledge.

Consistent with such experiences, Palmer writes about a different kind of knowledge that can be gained through service. This is significant for religious educators as it pertains to a spiritual knowledge that is born out of love. This kind of knowledge fosters deeper bonds and heals wounds. It is the kind of knowledge that emerges from compassion, which motivates the mind to know as an act of love. As Palmer explains, "Here, the act of knowing is an act of love, the act of entering and embracing the reality of the other, of allowing the other to enter and embrace our own. In such knowing, we know and are known as members of one community, and our knowing becomes a way of reweaving that community's bonds."[78] In other words, Palmer's curriculum of service flows out to repair the world.

CONCLUDING THOUGHTS

This chapter has focused on the contributions of Parker J. Palmer towards the field of religious education. One of the most significant contributions is Parker Palmer himself. As a public intellectual, he brings gifts to bear that can make him a bridge between religious traditions. He uses a language that is re-imaginative and captures the imagination of people. His language is non-ecclesiastical, a secular language to which people are receptive. As such, he is also a link between the secular and political arenas.

In this chapter, I examined Palmer's contributions in the context of the school classroom and the school environment. As a scholar, he brings together four themes that can alter the way one teaches, learns, and engages in the world. The themes are: living an integral and authentic life, the importance of community, teaching and learning for transformation, and nonviolent social change. These themes are applicable to religious education, given that its central theme is living in the presence of God. The chapter synthesizes Palmer's philosophy of teaching and learning through his spiritual perspective. This is articulated in his theory of pedagogy. The purpose of his theory is self-actualization. This calls forth in him an approach that is deeply spiritual and profoundly humanistic.

---

78. Palmer, *To Know as We Are Known*, 8.

Palmer's pedagogical theory is formulated as six paradoxes. Each is concerned with creating a sacred space in the classroom, which is an important element for religious educators: "(1) the space should be bounded and open, (2) the space should be hospitable and charged, (3) the space should invite the voice of the individual, and the voice of the group, (4) the space should honor the 'little' stories of the students, and the 'big' stories of the disciplines and traditions, (5) the space should provide community and solitude, and (6) the space should welcome both silence and speech."[79]

Together, the six paradoxes are important in holding the creative tension within the classroom space. Nonetheless, hospitality is the key element. Palmer defines hospitality as a space where one is received openly, with honor and care. He maintains that the classroom is optimally a space free of judgment, where in faith, together, truths will be uncovered in the authentic interaction between students and teacher.

The philosophy of Parker J. Palmer covers broad concepts. The concepts are woven throughout his theory of pedagogy. As such, his contributions to the field of religious education are examined across various curricula, all of which are in constant interplay with one another. They are the curriculum of the classroom, the curriculum of community, and the curriculum of service. Together, they articulate his primary purpose: teaching and learning for transformation.

In citing my own work experiences along with those of Stephen Lewis and Gregory Ellison II, what becomes evident is that there are instances where we could not fully engage Palmer's work because of the differences between our contexts and his, as a privileged white male who came of age in the mid-twentieth-century. However, his work is powerful and can be a way to move us forward. For example, Palmer writes about bridging divides and recalling and living the truths handed down to us through ancient traditions. This forms the essence of bridging the racial divide in our country as well as dismantling the oppressive system created by white privilege. In the current climate, our work, it seems, is to encourage people to want to enter into dialogue. Schools and churches are the most obvious places to build upon this work and challenge the structures that have not only created walls, but that have functioned to maintain their existence.

In a more immediate sense, schools can work to encourage dialogue among their faculty to build a better teaching community—one that has not only the students' but the teacher's interests at heart. This can be done

---

79. Palmer, *Courage to Teach*, 76–77.

through continual engagements that bring faculty and administrators together at a more personal level. Perhaps as Ellison and Lewis have done, Palmer's work can be applied to the school as a community, as opposed to individual teachers' and administrators' work. And, perhaps these efforts could be pursued not under the guise of professional development, but as a spiritual formation process that aims not only to get the teachers and administrators in touch with what they need to do to transform the school community, but to move them into action towards that goal. To use Lewis' example, teachers and administrators need to be challenged to take small steps at least, with "their most faithful step in what it is they have discerned [about] what they have been called to do."

From a practical sense, engaging the school as a community with the goal of re-imagining it as a place where there is caring, mutual support, and trust would require that the impetus either come from or is strongly supported by the school leaders. Usually, such change happens when like-minded leaders find each other and begin to construct ideas of how to effect this kind of change. It would be similar to school leaders having the kinds of conversations that Palmer has on his back porch with other leaders and teachers who share a vision for change. Then, as Lewis suggests, they would go out and begin prototyping it and embodying it in their schools. These school leaders would need to be individuals who, in Howard Thurman's description, "come alive" with the idea of doing this work.

As I have maintained in this book, Parker Palmer offers theories and practices that religious educators could use as the key to unlock some of the treasures that schools have to offer. Religious educators could potentially become the ideal body of leaders who, working collectively, have the potential to usher in the needed change in schools. Their work, which is grounded in the earthly mission of God, is fertile ground for creating an environment that students could call home: a hospitable school environment where there is mutual trust and where one's truth can be uncovered. School could become sacred space, where students and faculty can be their authentic selves, created in the image and likeness of God.

The findings in his work mark Parker Palmer as one of the most influential public intellectuals and educators of his time. Moreover, his work informs the work of religious educators about how most effectively to engage students to help form them into the individuals that they were created to be.

BIBLIOGRAPHY

Bamberger, John Eudes. "The Monk." In *Thomas Merton, Monk: A Monastic Tribute*, edited by Patrick Hart, 39–60. New York: Image, 1976.
Barone, Tom, and Elliot Eisner. "Arts-Based Educational Research." In *Complementary Methods for Research in Education*, edited by Richard M. Jaeger, 73–82. Washington, DC: American Educational Research Association, 1997.
Black, Susan. "A Lifeboat for New Teachers." *The American School Board Journal* 188 (2001) 46–48.
Boys, Mary C. *Educating in Faith*. Lima, OH: Academic, 1989.
Buber, Martin. *Tales of the Hasidim: The Early Masters*. New York: Schocken, 1975.
Buechner, Frederick. *Wishful Thinking: A Seeker's ABC*. San Francisco: Harper: San Francisco, 1993.
Bushnell, Horace. *Christian Nurture*. New Haven, CT: Yale University Press, 1967.
Coe, George Albert. *Education in Religion of a Mature Mind*. Chicago: Revell, 1902.
———. *Education in Religion and Morals*. New York: Revell, 1904.
Creswell, John W. *Qualitative Inquiry and Research Design: Choosing Among Five Traditions*. Thousand Oaks, CA: SAGE, 1998.
Cunningham, William G., and J. Brent Sperry. "The Underpaid Educator." *The American School Board Journal* 188 (2001) 38–42.
Day, Dorothy. *The Long Loneliness: An Autobiography*. New York: Harper & Row, 1952.
Denzin, Norman K. *Interpretive Biography*. Newbury Park, CA: SAGE, 1989.
Dewey, John. *A Common Faith*. New Haven, CT: Yale University Press, 1934.
———. *Democracy and Education*. New York: Macmillan, 1916.
———. "My Pedagogic Creed." In *Dewey on Education,* edited by Martin Dworkin, 19–32. Classics in Education 3. New York: Columbia University Teacher's College Press, 1959.
———. *Reconstruction in Philosophy*. Boston: Beacon, 1957.
———. "Religion and Our Schools." In *Characters and Events,* edited by Joseph Ratner, 2:514–17. New York: Henry Holt, 1929.
———. "The School and Society." In *Dewey on Education,* edited by Martin Dworkin, 33–49. Classics in Education 3. New York: Columbia University Teacher's College Press, 1959.

Bibliography

Dickinson, Emily. *The Poems of Emily Dickinson: Reading Edition.* Cambridge, MA: The Belknap Press of Harvard University Press, 1998.

Dillard, Annie. *Teaching a Stone to Talk.* New York: HarperCollins, 1982.

DuBois, W. E. B. *The Souls of Black Folks.* New York: Dover, 1994.

Edgerton, Russell. "Filling the Void." *Change* 19 (1987) 9–11.

Eisner, Elliot W. *The Educational Imagination: On the Design and Evaluation of School Programs.* Upper Saddle River: Merrill Prentice Hall, 2002.

Eliot, T. S. "Four Quartets: Little Gidding." In *The Complete Poems and Plays*, 145. New York: Harcourt, 1952.

Ellison, Gregory, II. Interview by Elena Soto. Video conference, May 11, 2019. Esquith, Rafe. *Real Talk for Real Teachers.* New York: Penguin, 2014.

Floden, Robert, et al. "A Nation at Risk or a Nation in Progress? Naming the Way Forward Through Research." *Journal of Teacher Education* 71 (2020) 169–71.

Fox, Matthew. *The Reinvention of Work.* New York; Harper Collins, 1994.

Gadamer, Hans-Georg. "Hermeneutics and Social Science." *Cultural Hermeneutics* 2 (1975) 307–16.

———. "Practical Philosophy as a Model of the Human Sciences." *Research in Phenomenology* 9 (1979) 74–85.

———. *Truth and Method.* New York: Sheed and Ward London, 1989.

Goldstein, D. "School Reforms Fail to Lift U.S. on Global Test." The New York Times, December 3, 2019. https://www.nytimes.com/2019/12/03/us/us-students-international-test-scores.html.

Green, Elizabeth. *Building A+ Better Teacher: How Teaching Works.* New York: W.W. Norton, 2015.

Greene, Maxine. "A Philosopher Looks at Qualitative Research." In *Complementary Methods of Research in Education*, edited by Richard M. Jaeger, 189–205. Washington, DC: American Educational Research Association, 1997.

Groome, Thomas H. "Advice to Beginners—And to Myself." *Religious Education* 102 (2007) 362–66.

———. *Christian Religious Education: Sharing Our Story and Vision.* San Francisco: Jossey-Bass, 1980.

———. *Educating for Life: A Spiritual Vision for Every Teacher and Parent.* New York: Crossroad, 1998.

———. "The Spirituality of the Religious Educator." *Religious Education* 83 (1988) 9–20.

Gunn, Dennis. "Our Divided Society—A Challenge to Religious Education: REA's 1969 Convention and the Opening Up of Brave Conversations About Race and Religion." *Religious Education* 114 (2019) 214–26. https://www.tandfonline.com/doi/full/10.1080/00344087.2019.1608658.

Hare, Sally. Interview by Elena Soto, telephone call, May 16, 2011.

Harper, Ida Husted. *History of Woman Suffrage Volume 6 (1900–1920).* New York: New York Times, 1969.

Harren, Robert, and John F. Kinney. *Celebrating the Eucharist.* Collegeville, MN: Liturgical, 2013.

Harris, Maria, and Gabriel Moran. *Reshaping Religious Education: Conversations on Contemporary Practice.* Louisville, KY: Westminster John Knox, 1998.

Horell, Harold Daly. "Fostering Hope: Christian Religious Education in a Postmodern Age." *Religious Education* 99 (2004) 5–22.

———. "The Wisdom of Students, Educators for Peace and Justice, and Religious Education." *Religious Education* 105 (2010) 3–7.
Huebner, Dwayne E. "Curriculum . . . With Liberty and Justice for All." Paper presented at the Conference on Craft, Conflict and Symbols: Their Import for Curriculum and Schooling, Tennessee Technological University, April 25–26, 1974.
———. "Religious Metaphors in the Language of Education." In *The Lure of the Transcendent: Collected Essays by Dwayne E. Huebner*, edited by Vikki Hillis, 460–72. Mahwah, NJ: Lawrence Erlbaum Associates, 1985.
Intrator, Sam M. *Living the Questions: Essays Inspired by the Work and Life of Parker J. Palmer*. San Francisco: Jossey-Bass, 2005.
Jain, Arun Kumar. *Faith and Philosophy of Jainism*. New Delhi, India: Kalpaz, 2009.
Jonas, Robert A. "Introduction." In *Henri Nouwen*, xiii–lxix. Modern Spiritual Masters Series. Maryknoll, NY: Orbis, 1998.
Kelty, Matthew. "The Man." In *Thomas Merton, Monk: A Monastic Tribute*, edited by Patrick Hart, 21–37. New York: Image, 1976.
Keown, Damien. *Buddhism; A Very Short Introduction*. Oxford: Oxford University Press, 2013.
Knott, Kim. *Hinduism: A Very Short Introduction*. New York: Oxford University Press, 1998.
Lakeland, Paul. *Catholicism at the Crossroads: How the Laity Can Save the Church*. New York: Continuum, 2007.
Lama, Dalai. *The Heart of Meditation*. Boulder, CO: Shambhala, 2016.
Lampert, Magdalene. *Teaching Problems and the Problem of Teaching*. New Haven, CT: Yale University Press, 2001.
Lasch, Christopher. *The Culture of Narcissism: American Life in an Age of Diminishing Expectations*. New York: Norton, 1978.
"Leadership Project Award." *Change* (January-February 1998) 14.
Lentfoehr, Thérèse. "The Solitary." In *Thomas Merton, Monk: A Monastic Tribute*, edited by Patrick Hart, 61–80. New York: Image, 1976.
Leclerq, Jean. "The Evolving Monk." In *Thomas Merton, Monk: A Monastic Tribute*, edited by Patrick Hart, 93–104. New York: Image, 1976.
Levine, Arthur. *When Dreams and Heroes Died*. San Francisco: Jossey-Bass, 1981.
Lewis, Stephen. Interview by Elena Soto. Video conference, June 9, 2019.
Lewis, Stephen, et al. *Another Way Is Possible: Living and Leading Change on Purpose*. St. Louis: Chalice, 2020.
Liebsch, MegAnne. "Ignatian Family Cries Out for Racial Justice." *Jesuits*, June 10, 2020. https://www.jesuits.org/stories/ignatian-family-cries-out-for-racial-justice/.
Martin, James, SJ. *Becoming Who You Are: Insights on the True Self from Thomas Merton and Other Saints*. Mahwah, NJ: Hidden Spring, 2006.
Massingale, Bryan. "The Assumptions of White Privilege and What We Can Do about It." *National Catholic Reporter*, June 1, 2020. https://www.ncronline.org/news/opinion/assumptions-white-privilege-and-what-we-can-do-about-it.
Merton, Thomas. "Final Integration: Toward a 'Monastic Therapy.'" In *Contemplation in a World of Action*, 200–212. Notre Dame, IN: University of Notre Dame Press, 1998.
———. "Hagia Sophia." In *A Thomas Merton Reader*, edited by Thomas P. McDonnell, 506. New York: Doubleday, 1989.
———. *Love and Living*. New York: Bantam, 1979.
———. *New Seeds of Contemplation*. New York: New Directions, 1961.

Bibliography

Mezirow, Jack. *Transformative Dimensions of Adult Learning*. San Francisco: Jossey-Bass, 1991.

Modras, Ronald. *Ignatian Humanism: A Dynamic Spirituality for the 21st Century*. Chicago: Loyola, 2004.

Moran, Gabriel. *Education Toward Adulthood: Religion and Lifelong Learning*. New York: Paulist, 1979.

———. "Interest in Philosophy: Three Themes for Religious Education." *Religious Education* 81 (1986) 425–45.

———. *Religious Education as a Second Language*. Birmingham, AL: Religious Education, 1989.

———. *Showing How: The Act of Teaching*. Valley Forge, PA: Trinity, 1997.

Mullino Moore, Mary Elizabeth. *Teaching as a Sacramental Act*. Cleveland, OH: Pilgrim, 2004.

Neafsey, John. *A Sacred Voice Is Calling: Personal Vocation and Social Conscience*. New York: Orbis, 2009.

Nouwen, Henri. *Henri Nouwen*. Modern Spiritual Masters Series. Maryknoll, NY: Orbis, 1998.

———. *The Inner Voice of Love: A Journey through Anguish to Freedom*. New York: Doubleday, 1996.

———. *The Wounded Healer*. New York: Doubleday, 1972.

Oliver, Mary. "Maybe." In *The Soul Is Here for Its Own Joy: Sacred Poems from Many Cultures*, edited by Robert Bly, 15. Hopewell, NJ: Ecco, 1995.

Palmer, Parker J. *The Active Life: A Spirituality of Work, Creativity and Caring*. San Francisco: Jossey-Bass, 1990.

———. "All the Way Down: Depression and the Spiritual Journey." *Weavings* (September-October 1998) 31–41.

———. "Community, Conflict and Ways of Knowing: Ways to Deepen Our Educational Agenda." *Change* 19 (1987) 20–26.

———. *The Company of Strangers: Christians and the Renewal of America's Public Life*. New York: Crossroad, 1981.

———. *The Courage to Teach: Exploring the Inner Landscape of a Teacher's Life*. San Francisco: Jossey-Bass, 2007.

———. "A Great People to Be Gathered: The View from Pendle Hill." *Friends Journal*, June 11, 2011. http://www.friendsjournal.org/great-people-be-gathered-view-pendle-hill.

———. *Healing the Heart of Democracy: The Courage to Create a Politics Worthy of the Human Spirit*. San Francisco: Jossey-Bass, 2014.

———. *A Hidden Wholeness: The Journey toward an Undivided Life*. San Francisco: Jossey-Bass, 2004.

———. Interview by Elena Soto. Madison, Wisconsin, April 5, 2010.

———. Interview by Elena Soto. Telephone call, April 29, 2019.

———. *Let Your Life Speak: Listening for the Voice of Vocation*. San Francisco: Jossey-Bass, 2000.

———. "Meeting for Learning: Education in a Quaker Context." Wallingford, PA: Pendle Hill: Philadelphia: Friends Council on Education (1976) 3–25.

———. "On Minding Your Call—When No One is Calling." *Weavings* (May-June 1996) 15–22.

———. *On the Brink of Everything: Grace, Gravity, and Getting Old*. Oakland, CA: Berrett-Koehler, 2018.

———. *The Promise of Paradox: A Celebration of Contradictions in the Christian Life.* San Francisco: Jossey-Bass, 2008.

———. *Seeking Vocation in Darkness and Light.* Swannanoa, NC: Warren College, 1999.

———. *To Know as We Are Known: Education as a Spiritual Journey.* New York: HarperCollins, 1983.

———. "Transforming Teaching and Learning in Higher Education: An Interview with Parker J. Palmer." *Spirituality in Higher Education Newsletter* 5 (2009) 1–9.

———. "The Violence of Our Knowledge: Toward a Spirituality of Higher Education." 1993. http://www.kairos2.com/palmer_1999.htm.

Pennington, M. Basil. *Thomas Merton, My Brother: His Journey to Freedom, Compassion, and Final Integration.* New York: New City, 1996.

Pew Research Center. "Measuring Religion in Pew Research Center's American Trends Panel." January 14, 2021. https://www.pewresearch.org/religion/2021/01/14/measuring-religion-in-pew-research-centers-american-trends-panel/.

Pinar, William F. *Race, Religion, and a Curriculum of Reparation: Teacher Education for a Multicultural Society.* New York: Palgrave MacMillan, 2006.

Rolheiser, Ronald. *The Holy Longing: The Search for a Christian Spirituality.* New York: Doubleday, 1999.

Rourke, John. "The Power of Paradox: How High School Teachers Perceive the Navigation of Paradox Influencing Teacher Resiliency and Student Motivation." PhD diss., Johnson & Wales University, 2010.

Rudy, Willis. "Josiah Royce and the Art of Teaching." *Educational Theory* 2 (1952) 158–69.

Salazar, Maria. "Interrogating Teacher Evaluation: Unveiling Whiteness as the Normative Center and Moving Margins." *Journal of Teacher Education* 69 (2018) 463–76.

Sarton, May. "Now I Become Myself." In *Collected Poems, 1930–1993,* 162. New York: Norton, 1993.

Scott, Kieran. "Moving Beyond the Sound of Silence." In *Human Sexuality in the Catholic Tradition,* edited by Kieran Scott and Harold Daly Horell, 3–12. Lanham, MD: Rowman & Littlefield, 2007.

Shea, John J. *Finding God Again.* Lanham, MD: Rowman & Littlefield, 2005.

Shenk, Joshua W. *Lincoln's Melancholy.* New York: Houghton Mifflin, 2005.

Spiller, Chellie, et al. *Wayfinding Leadership.* Wellington, New Zealand: Huia, 2015.

Steindl-Rast, David. "Man of Prayer." In *Thomas Merton, Monk: A Monastic Tribute,* edited by Patrick Hart, 81–90. New York: Image, 1976.

Talvacchia, Kathleen T. *Critical Minds and Discerning Hearts: A Spirituality of Multicultural Teaching.* St. Louis: Chalice, 2003.

Underwood, Kenneth, ed. *The Church, the University, and Social Policy.* Middletown, CT: Wesleyan University Press, 1969.

Walker, Decker F., and Jonas F. Soltis. *Curriculum and Aims.* New York: Teachers College Press, 2004.

Wong, Eva. *Taoism: An Essential Guide.* Boston: Shambhala, 2011.